UNIQUE GHOST TOWNS

and

MOUNTAIN SPOTS

The Author

D.K.P., 1960

Caroline Bancroft is a third generation Coloradan who began writing her first history for *The Denver Post* in 1928.

Her long-standing interest in western history was inherited. Her pioneer grandfather, Dr. F. J. Bancroft, was a founder of the Colorado Historical Society and its first president.

His granddaughter has carried on the family tradition. She is the author of the interesting series of Bancroft Booklets, *Silver Queen: T h e Fabulous Story of Baby Doe Tabor, Famous Aspen, Denver's Lively Past, Historic Central City, The Brown Palace in Denver, Tabor's Matchless Mine and Lusty Leadville, Augusta Tabor: Her Side of the Scandal, Glenwood's Early Glamor, Colorado's Lost Gold Mines and Buried Treasure, The Unsinkable Mrs. Brown* and *Colorful Colorado.*

A Bachelor of Arts from Smith College, she later obtained a Master of Arts degree from the University of Denver, writing her thesis on Central City, Colorado. Her full-size *Gulch of Gold* is the definitive history of that well-known area, which includes Nevadaville, the scene of the accompanying photo. She is shown with Daniel K. Peterson who drew the maps and took most of the contemporary pictures for the new booklet on ghost towns.

STEPHEN L. R. McNICHOLS
Governor of Colorado
1956-1962

The Cover

The Dumont boarding house in North Empire, unique for its ground-level dormer windows, was built about 1872 for miners working on the Benton lode, owned by John M. Dumont. In 1897, with a date still on the wall, it was bought by a Mrs. Bishop who painted the building a purplish blue. She operated it as a boarding house until about 1906 when she took over the Peck House (Hotel Splendide) in Empire. Still later, in the 1930's, Waldemar Nelson lived in the "Blue House" and used one section as a machine shop. A forge was still there in 1960. Photo by Dan Peterson.

UNIQUE
GHOST TOWNS
and
MOUNTAIN SPOTS

CAROLINE BANCROFT
Assisted by
DANIEL K. PETERSON

JOHNSON BOOKS
Boulder, Colorado

Personal to the Reader

I love the high country of Colorado—and in a less effusive manner, so does Dan Peterson. Partly for your enjoyment and partly for our own, this booklet represents the crystallization of our mutual enthusiasms. We hope that it will serve as a useful guide for you and others who thrill to the heights and diverse grandeur of our Colorado Rockies.

But first, a word of warning: if after reading this booklet, you add one act of vandalism, or carelessly cast one burning cigarette to the winds, or messily leave a beer can in a crystal creek bed, the whole purpose of our publication has been defeated. We have written about ghost towns out of love of their dramatic past and a reverence for their present fragility. If you follow in our footsteps to these mountain spots, we entreat you to go in the same spirit.

When I said this booklet represented a "crystallization" of our mutual enthusiasms, I could not have spoken more truly. Dan is still "hurting," as he phrases it, because Gladstone, his favorite ghost town, had to be left out due to limitations of space. In order to appease his hurt, I have agreed that he can sneak in its location on the Silverton map and a short paragraph of description in the text.

And what have I had to sacrifice? Too many pets, such as Beartown, reminder of the brave history of Stony and Hunchback Passes; Mineral Point and its lonely sentinel, the San Juan Chief shaft house still perched across a fork of Poughkeepsie Gulch and seen as one jeeps up to thrilling Engineer Pass, and Mayday, where I have never been but am intrigued by its romantic sound.

Our booklet does offer you forty-two "ghost towns" in photograph and story, plus passing mention on a map or in the text of a few others. These forty-two are reached from twenty-two attractive mountain towns where it is possible to obtain good accommodations. All but three of our final choices may be visited by ordinary car. For Lulu City, you will have to walk a three-mile trail or ride a horse; for Bachelor, you may take your car most of the way but will have to walk the last mile or jeep the whole distance, and for Carson, you will have to go by jeep or horse from Lake City. For the most part our forty-two towns are easy to see and in their separate ways unique.

Here, another word of warning: there are almost no ghost towns any more. In the true sense of the word they are gone. If you had been able to ride a horse or were willing to punish your Model T Ford, I could have taken you in the 1920's to dozens of true ghost towns no farther away than along the Front Range. Even in the late 1940's, when jeeps first came in, I could still have guided you to many true ghost towns. But no more.

What has happened? Tourists (a mixed blessing) and natives who have no regard for Colorado's appealing past, have stolen from them, vandalized them, destroyed buildings, and carted whole towns away. Another killer in the form of fierce high-country winters has levelled them under tons of heavy white snow or pulled them apart with snatching, tearing wind. Whether desecrated by humans or eroded by nature, I am constantly reminded of Charles Kingsley's lines, painted on the Tabor Grand Theatre curtain:

So fleet the works of men, back to the earth again,
Ancient and holy things fade like a dream.

In other cases the ghost towns have undergone a metamorphosis. Some settlements have changed into summer resorts because of the charm of their buildings or the picturesqueness of their settings. Sometimes their ghost town status was lost by a new industry moving in, such as the sawmill at Lenado; or a new motor road has been strategically built, such as the Peak-to-Peak Highway which redeemed Ward. These towns, although peopled only by ghosts for many years, once again throb with life today. Many of the summer-resort group are alive only in the warm months. When the aspens have lost their fluttering gold in the autumn, they return to ghost towns.

We have included some of each type. All were true ghost towns once, and all had ghostly reminders still extant in 1960. But if you, as you visit them, should fail to leave everything as you find it, there will soon be nothing left for anyone to see. A sad and forlorn example of what can happen in only a short time is the formerly beautiful Lee House at Capitol City. When I first saw it in 1955, the house was still a true mansion, and its atmosphere eerily evoked the great and pretentious dreams of its builder. But in 1960 despoiling tourists had changed it to a horrid ruin.

So go forth in the true spirit of adventure to see and to enjoy, and may this little book add to your enjoyment!

A plan for touring the whole state and a large folded-in map of Colorado serve as introduction to the special towns and separate tours that follow. On the large map, the towns suggested for starting points are shown as black dots and are numbered to correspond with the numbers of the individual tours. The ghost towns appear as red dots. On the smaller maps the starting points are shown as squares, and the ghost towns as solid circles. Dan has drawn them all with the double purpose of being accurate and helpfully clear.

But however clear the plan and maps, real enjoyment in visiting these sites can only be had if the viewer has adequate knowledge of the people who built these towns and the times they lived in. Before setting out on the trips recommended here, some general knowledge of the state's history is a *must*. To this end no quicker method exists than a reading of *Colorful Colorado,* a good companion volume.

The photographs, employed throughout the present booklet as illustrations, carry credit lines which should be plain to all except where initials have been used. DKP stands for Daniel K. Peterson; CHS, for Colorado Historical Society, and DPL, for the Western History Collection of the Denver Public Library.

My own part in the production of this work needs no explanation. My first visit to a ghost town was in 1904 when, as a toddler, I was carried on horseback by my father to Alice (then a thriving little spot). Alice was my father's headquarters for building a reservoir system from five high mountain lakes that emptied into a sixth. These lakes (one, *Lake Caroline*) lie some four to six miles beyond Alice.

Since that distant day I have never ceased to travel to Colorado's mountain towns, and I frequently describe myself as a "hillbilly." No matter where I have been, it has always been the mountains of faraway lands that have had the greatest drawing power for me—the Jotunheim range of Norway, the Highlands of Scotland, the Alps in France and Switzerland, the Apennines in Italy and the Himalayas in India.

Yes, I can say along with Keats:

Much have I travelled in the realms of gold,
And many goodly state and kingdoms seen . . .

* * *

Yet none speaks so well of romance untold
As our high ghostly towns, still and serene.

THE ALICE POST OFFICE STILL STANDS

George J. Bancroft, 1904; D.P.L.

PLAN OF TOURS

TOUR No.	STARTING POINT	GHOST TOWNS AND MOUNTAIN SPOTS	PAGE
1.	CENTRAL CITY	Nevadaville, American City, Kingston	8
2.	IDAHO SPRINGS	Alice, North Empire	14
3.	GEORGETOWN	Waldorf, Sts. John	20
4.	BOULDER	Caribou	24
5.	ESTES PARK	Ward	26
6.	GRAND LAKE	Lulu City	28
7.	STEAMBOAT SPRINGS	Hahns Peak	32
8.	GLENWOOD SPRINGS	Fulford, Crystal City	34
9.	ASPEN	Lenado, Ashcroft	40
10.	LEADVILLE	Independence, Stumptown	44
11.	FAIRPLAY	Buckskin Joe, Como, Mudsill, Leavick	48
12.	CRIPPLE CREEK	Altman, Bull Hill Station, Goldfield	52
13.	CANON CITY	Rosita, Silver Cliff	56
14.	SALIDA	Turret, Bonanza	59
15.	BUENA VISTA	St. Elmo, Winfield	63
16.	GUNNISON	Tin Cup, Gothic	66
17.	LAKE CITY	Capitol City, Carson	70
18.	CREEDE	Spar City, Bachelor	75
19.	DEL NORTE	Summitville	82
20.	SILVERTON	Eureka, Animas Forks	84
21.	OURAY	Red Mountain, Ironton	88
22.	TELLURIDE	Pandora	92

From Central City

Nevadaville is unique for many reasons. It was part of the historic 1859 "Pikes Peak or Bust" gold rush. In 1861 the town was larger than Denver. In 1863 one of Nevadaville's mines, the Pat Casey (later the Ophir), was sold by its illiterate Irish owner in New York to Wall Street speculators for a fancy sum which started a boom in Gilpin County mines. Stock shares of Nevadaville's mines were thus the first of Colorado corporations to be quoted on the "big board."

When John H. Gregory found the first lode gold of Colorado in Gregory Gulch on May 6, 1859, other prospectors immediately pushed up all the tributary gulches. By the latter part of May a number of good claims had been staked on Quartz Hill above Nevada Creek. This creek joins Spring Creek at Central City and together they join Eureka Creek to make the mile-long Gregory Creek. It, in turn, joins the North Fork of Clear Creek at Black Hawk. The closest source of water for the mines on Quartz Hill was Nevada Creek. A camp sprang up immediately, and was named Nevada City.

A great deal of confusion followed this naming. Some referred to it only as Nevada and some as Nevadaville. When the townspeople petitioned for a post office they were given Bald Mountain because of a similarity with Nevada City, California. Nevertheless, increasingly through the years, the residents continued to call it Nevadaville and few people today know of its other names.

The earliest good finds were the Illinois by John Gregory, the Burroughs by Benjamin Burroughs and his brother, and the Casey (or Ophir) by Pat Casey. The Burroughs and Pat Casey were among the founders of Nevadaville.

8

The town had a long and boisterous life. It was settled largely by Cornish at the western end and by Irish at the eastern. These two groups waged a prolonged and skull-cracking battle with each other until the 1890's. Then they found it expedient to unite against an influx from the Tyrol of miners who threatened to undercut their wages.

The Cornish (Cousin Jacks) built two charming little churches, an Episcopalian and a Methodist. (Both are now gone.) The Irish drove or walked down to mass at St. Mary's-of-the-Assumption in Central City, over a mile away. But however earnest their church attendance on Sunday morning, it never altered their beer drinking at Nevadaville's thirteen saloons that afternoon nor the fights and murders that followed. Two of the latter, both Cousin Jacks killed by Irishmen, were notorious in the annals of Colorado law and were eventually carried to the Supreme Court.

I have told the town's story at considerable length in *Gulch of Gold* to which the reader is referred for rollicking details. Nevadaville's ghost status began in 1920 and worsened for twenty-five years. On the bleak scrubby side of Nevada Hill more and more buildings fell down or were torn down. By World War II only two permanent residents remained, and finally there were none.

Nevadaville, similar to all gold camps in Colorado, had a renascence during the 1930's when the price of gold rose from $20 an ounce to $35. During this period a number of its mines were re-opened in-

NEVADAVILLE HAD THIRTEEN SALOONS

This view looks northeast across Nevada Creek to the main street, which continues at the right on down to Central City and Denver.

A. M. Thomas, 1900; D.P.L.

CORNISH COTTAGES COVERED THIS SLOPE

The population of Nevadaville was twelve hundred in 1900 when the upper photo was taken. The Union Bakery wagon was delivering bread and pastries; an ore wagon was heading up toward Alps Hill, and a number of residents, both on this side of Nevada Creek and the other, were interested in the photographer's work. In 1960 no one was around to be curious; the lower bridge was gone, but the slopes were the same.

D.K.P., 1960

cluding the Hubert, which was worked by Frankie Warren. Frankie was one of the delightful Cousin Jacks left from the old days and could tell dialect stories by the dozens. I spent a number of delightful evenings in Nevadaville listening to his reminiscences and was particularly amused by his 'ant' (haunt) stories. One of these was about the Bald Mountain cemetery (a charming spot west of the settlement and worth a side trip) where the parents of Estel Slater had installed his photo on his tombstone and covered it with glass. On moonlight nights a ghost moved in the cemetery. Frankie went up to investigate and discovered the reflected light. I, too, followed Frankie's example and was startled by the effect—I hope they are still there for you to see. There is always the danger that they have been vandalized. But let us return to Nevadaville.

Of recent years hardy souls who did not mind coping with the meagre water supply have renovated the remaining houses. In 1960 parts of Nevadaville presented a spruce appearance. But the mines which were once rich and storied, contributing a large part of Gilpin County's $106,000,000 production, are ruins. The ghostliness that they cast and the derelict Main Street were little affected by the neat cottages. It does not take much imagination on a still afternoon to hear a Cornish "tommy-knocker" or to see why Nevadaville rates first among the ghost towns . . .

Farther on toward the continental divide, past Apex and a sign erroneously marked *Private Road,* is American City. A mixture of occupied and deserted buildings, the town lies hidden on the wooded side of Colorado Mountain overlooking a glen. A number of the deserted cabins and pretty sites may be bought from the county for back taxes. But others are in fine repair and lovingly cared for. Be wary in American City not to cast yourself in the role of "trespasser."

American City's history is not long and dramatic like Nevadaville's. But its story is unique for glamor, gayety and culture. After the crash of silver in 1893, desperate efforts were made to find as yet undiscovered gold, and new strikes were made in the Pine Creek Mining District of Gilpin County. By 1895 Apex had reached sufficient stature to be listed in the Colorado Business Directory, as the district's principal town, having two hotels and a general merchandise store. By June 1896 the *Denver Times* was saying, "American City is very dressy."

A year later the *Denver Republican* described the main stockholders of the American Company who were from Illinois and Iowa. It added that this company was in good financial condition, was running two shifts of miners and had opened a library in their office in American City which "now numbers 503 books and the miners appreciate the courtesy on the part of the company."

11

D.K.P., 1960

AMERICAN CITY HUGS THE TREES

The mill (which was built by a master carpenter of the German ship-yards) was in ruins, but the Hotel del Monte (second in the trees) stood.

On July 3, 1897, a newspaper called the *Pine Cone* began publication at Apex and carried frequent delightful items about American City. Captain E. M. Stedman, one of the principal stockholders, was also manager. On April 28, 1900, it reported that he was becoming an expert at "skeeing" since "he made the distance on Tuesday from his residence in American City to Apex, about a mile and a half, in five minutes."

One of American City's proudest possessions was its mill built by Gus Meyer in 1903. Meyer was a master craftsman from Germany and did contract work in Denver. He was the boss carpenter on the Barth Block. Because of his excellent work on the business building, William Barth gave him $100 in gold coin in addition to his contract money.

In the succeeding years up to around 1910 the Stedmans frequently entertained at house parties, using their own palatial cabin and overflowing into the cabins of other Eastern stockholders as well as the Hotel del Monte. My mother and father were present at a number of these affairs, and I can remember the fuss of getting all the luggage packed with a correct riding habit and a number of evening gowns for Mother to dress for dinner. It was indeed a glamorous place.

12

Then the gold petered out, and American City was abandoned. For years it was almost lost to view and to memory. Only the late wealthy Mrs. John Anthony Crook maintained a summer cabin there. In the 1930's she was the lone resident. Finally a few others followed her lead until the town was partly saved . . .

Nugget, on the way to Kingston, had a few remnants in 1960. But uncared for, the fierce elements were wreaking havoc on the buildings as they also were at Kingston. The havoc was more serious at Kingston because of the beauty of the dormer-windowed boardinghouse close to the London mill and mine and because of the unusual latticed log cabin down on Secreto Creek at what is humorously called South Kingston.

In the late 1890's and early 1900's there were many residences along the ridge that runs between Pile Hill and Kingston Peak, and down the banks of Mosquito Creek. In 1960 some of these were still partially standing and many of their foundations were intact; but all were deteriorating fast. Kingston, like American City, was purely a mining, milling and residential town and depended on Apex for commerce, merchandise and a newspaper. But the details of its history are lost. Kingston is unique because of its mystery.

KINGSTON IS IN TWO SECTIONS

Shown are the London boardinghouse, mill and mine (far right). More miners lived down in Secreto Gulch to the left of this high ridge.

D.K.P., 1960

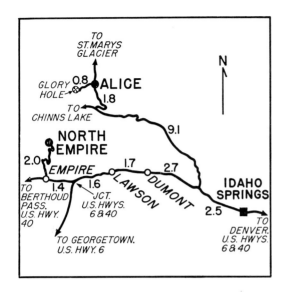

Alice was rich in gold—particularly placer gold. But oddly and uniquely, no one found these placers until long after other Clear Creek placers had been worked out. Apparently no prospector was thorough enough in his search on upper Fall River and its little tributary, Silver Creek, to make a strike during the placer excitements of 1859 and the early 1860's, although some silver was uncovered. When rich gold was finally found in 1881, the discovery was made by a party working west from Yankee along the road that ran from Central City, the county seat of Gilpin County, past the side of Yankee Hill, down Silver Creek and Fall River, and on to Georgetown, county seat of Clear Creek County.

Alice was described in Denver's *Rocky Mountain News* August 24, 1881, as a colony of fifteen or twenty tents near Silver City, a camp slightly higher up Silver Creek. Colonel A. J. Cropsey of Nebraska was the superintendent of the Alice Mining Company, and he was banking sums of twelve and fifteen hundred dollars every two weeks in the First National Bank at Central City.

The summer and fall production proved so successful that the following February the capital stock of the company was increased from $1,000,000 to $2,000,000; a second ditch was built to bring water for hydraulic mining; log cabins and a mill were erected; the eleven-mile road to Idaho Springs was improved, and the company banked $2,500 or $3,000 in Idaho Springs every fortnight.

Hydraulic mining continued through the early 1880's and proved consistently profitable so that Alice absorbed Silver City (if it had ever been anything more than a cluster of tents). As the placers were worked out, lode mining developed in a number of mines, especially in tunnels

14

that led away from a pit torn out by hydraulic hoses. The population was around thirty-five until after 1903 when it rose to fifty or sixty. In 1908 a more modern mill was built, and production continued steadily until 1915 when the mill shut down. Soon the ghosts took over.

Four people lingered on, including the E. J. Harpers. He had been postmaster in 1904 (see the photo at the end of my introduction) and had conducted business from one end of their own cabin. She served meals at the other. On inspection trips to the Loch Lomond reservoir my father and I used to tie our horses outside this cabin and have a delicious lunch. In 1960 it was being used as a summer cottage but its exterior lines were identical with Father's 1904 photo.

In 1934 Alice, like many other Colorado gold camps, experienced a renascence. (This was because of the price of gold rising from $20 to $35 an ounce.) The sturdy log cabins were re-roofed; the mill started, and the pit was turned into a real glory hole. Today Alice is unique because of its abandoned glory hole—the only summer resort-ghost town to boast of one within its town limits . . .

Returning to Clear Creek and driving farther up its course, is another tumbling tributary, a creek also coming in from the north. Originally this creek was called Lyon's, but now Lion. It flows through the town of Empire about which the splendid historian, Ovando J. Hollister, said in 1866, "Of all the towns brought into existence by the famed Cherry Creek Sands, Empire bears away the palm for a pretty location and picturesque surroundings." This statement is particularly true of North Empire, about a mile and a half up Lion Creek and its fork, North Empire Creek.

Bayard Taylor (the renowned nineteenth century lecturer and travel writer) and William N. Byers, founder and editor of the *Rocky Mountain News,* also visited the two towns that same year and were much impressed with their settings. Byers reported North Empire as "a hustling busy little hamlet right amid the mines. It has three or four mills."

He also mentioned by name a number of prosperous mines, especially the Atlantic owned by Frank Peck who was later the founder of Lower Empire's Peck House (now the Hotel Splendide). Byers was interested by an arastra in the gulch which was operated by water power and "was pointed out as a paying institution."

Lower Empire was organized in the spring of 1860 by a band of prospectors who came up from Spanish Bar (then on the south side of Clear Creek close to its junction with Fall River). The first gold was discovered on Eureka Mountain, northwest of Empire. A find of rich placers and lodes soon followed on Silver Mountain, north of Empire. It was these mines that caused North Empire to spring up on the side of Silver and the flanking mountainside to the east, Covode.

15

Too late to alter: now proved to be Russell Gulch.   E. S. Bastin, 1911; U.S.G.S.

ALICE BOASTED OF ITS GLORY HOLE

In 1911 two mills, the Anchor and Princess Alice, and six mining companies were operating when this view was taken. It looks southwest along the road that runs past the Glory Hole and eventually to the Loch Lomond Reservoir system, built and owned by G. J. Bancroft in the early 1900's. The 1960 view of the Glory Hole shows three roads at upper right: two up to Yankee and St. Mary's Glacier, and one off to Idaho Springs.

D.K.P., 1960

George Wakely, circa 1868; D.P.L.

NORTH EMPIRE CLUNG CLOSE TO THE MINES

The town was built on the side of Covode Mountain nearly opposite the Silver Mountain mining properties and equidistant between the two boardinghouse relics, the Dumont and the Conqueror. The 1960 shot of the Copper Cone (or Gold Fissure) mine was taken from approximately the same location, but looking north rather than east. The various levels of streets and a few foundations may still be seen through the trees.

D.K.P., 1960

North Empire led a prosperous existence during the 1860's and '70's but died out during the 1880's. Then in 1890 John M. Dumont, who had made money at Mill City (now Dumont after him) and Freeland, bought the Benton lode (named for Thomas Benton, the mountain man). Dumont attempted a resurrection of the town. The collapse of silver in 1893 added momentum to his efforts, and North Empire enjoyed a lively life for over a decade.

Again it was left to the blue jays and mountain rats until the 1930's when once more the mines and mills throbbed. When World War II drafted its miners, the mills shut down and the mine shafts filled with water. The town died forever—or until the price of gold again changes.

Nonetheless, the picturesqueness of North Empire's setting, commented on by all, lives on. The view to the south over Empire and Clear Creek to the meadow made by Bard Creek, on over Union Pass to the valley where Georgetown lies hidden, and on up to Guanella Pass against the skyline, is unsurpassed for its soft charm. North Empire remains unique for its picturesqueness.

THE CONQUEROR'S MINERS LIVED WELL

The south wing of the Conqueror's boardinghouse was built by W. S. Pryor in 1910. The original wing (at the right) dates from the 1870's. Unfortunately, vandals have since burned down this picturesque relic.

D.K.P., 1960

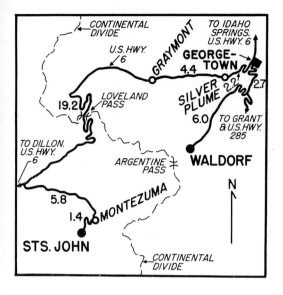

From Georgetown

Waldorf is unique because, single-handed, it was caused and named by a mining magnate who built his own little railroad—the Argentine Central—to create the town.

Edward John Wilcox was another of the many colorful characters Colorado has produced. He was full of quirks and idiosyncrasies. A former Methodist minister, he decided he could serve the church better by making money and tithing than by staying on with any of his former parishes in Longmont, Denver or Pueblo. Success attended his decision, and by 1905 he was the owner of some sixty-five mines on Leavenworth Mountain, south of Georgetown. But the mines were high in the East Argentine district where it was difficult to transport machinery in and ore out.

So on August 1 (Colorado Day), 1905, Wilcox began building his railroad, starting over eight miles away at Silver Plume and planning to grade switchbacks over Pendleton Mountain, the western wing of Leavenworth. By Colorado Day of the next year, the railroad had reached nearly eight miles beyond Waldorf to a point almost at the top of Mount McClellan. A second ceremony was held which included driving a gold spike. (The first had been held on reaching Waldorf.) Immediately afterward trains began operating to haul freight and tourists. But not on Sunday. Wilcox would not degrade the Lord's day!

A post office was opened in Waldorf at 11,666 feet in altitude claiming to be the highest in the United States, and Waldorf was prepared for a great future. It had already had a considerable past, if not under the name of Waldorf. The silver mines in both the West and East Argentine districts had been working since 1866 and been supporting two mills. One mill and a camp called Argentine (from the Latin word for silver, *argentum*) were fairly high in Leavenworth Gulch on the way to Argentine Pass. Their location was beside the stagecoach road from Georgetown to Montezuma. But now a large boardinghouse, several residences, a store and a depot clustered about the Waldorf and Vidler tunnels and their mills. Thus the new camp of Waldorf was born.

Everything went well at first for the town and railroad—even despite the ban on Sunday tourists. The little railroad made a great impression, and Wilcox was as proud as a racehorse stable owner as he added little Shay engines to his rolling stock. Early in 1907 a British syndicate offered $3,000,000 for his holdings around Waldorf including the railroad. Wilcox refused despite the enormous profit involved.

But 1907 turned out to be a bad year. A depression started gathering momentum in the East. During the last six months of the year the price of silver fell thirteen cents, and Waldorf ore was not worth hauling. By 1908 Wilcox was badly in debt and was forced to liquidate where he could. According to the railroad historians, Elmer O. Davis and Frank Hollenback, Wilcox sold his $300,000 railroad for $44,000. The new management took over in 1909 and made a bid for the tourist trade which naturally included trains on Sunday.

Still the railroad did not pay, and was sold again in 1912. Ironically, the buyer was William Rogers of Georgetown, the same Rogers who had suggested the idea of the railroad to Wilcox in the first place. Now he had his railroad all built and operating for only $19,500! Rogers founded a new company.

But the mines had never come back after the blow of '07. The tourist trade was not adequate to support the railroad with no freight to haul other than coal for the power company's maintenance station at Waldorf. The last Shay engines were sold in 1914, and gasoline engined cars replaced them. Even this drastic measure did not suffice. The income for the 1917 summer season was too lean for the company to continue. In 1920 permission was granted for abandonment, and the next year track was taken up.

Waldorf was truly dead. Since then, from time to time, assorted lessees have operated the Waldorf tunnel and the Santiago mine northwest of Waldorf on the side of Mount McClellan. While they were working, they took over some of the old buildings for a year or two as residences. In the 1950's Waldorf had two bad fires which destroyed the last of the big buildings and the habitable dwellings. In desperation the man who was working the Santiago mine in 1958, erected a Quonset hut for his home.

It stands as a sad commentary on these high towns where water is so precious and the menace of fire, an ever-present reality. Most

L. C. McClure, 1905-11; D.P.L.

WALDORF WAS A RAILROAD MINING TOWN

The upper view was taken with a telescopic lens and shows the Vidler mill in the foreground, the track from Vidler tunnel and one of its ore cars to the right, a team of horses to the left, and at Waldorf proper, a railroad coach and a boxcar on a siding. In both photos the road around to the Santiago mine and its power line across the hill are prominent. The Argentine Pass horseback trail goes off to the left.

D.K.P., 1960

Colorado mining camps have experienced terrible fires more than once, and Waldorf is no exception.

The hut's shiny newness makes Waldorf unique for still another reason—our only ghost town with a Quonset hut! . . .

To reach Saints John, less than eight miles away as the crow flies, you have to take a long circuitous route. But it is a scenic ride, and the pastoral seclusion of Saints John should be worth the trip. The town lies between Glacier Mountain on the southeast and Bear Mountain on the northwest. It snuggles along the banks of Saints John Creek which runs into the Snake River at Montezuma. At the head of Saints John Creek is Bear Pass which leads over into the Swan River, a tributary of the Blue, and on to Breckenridge.

It was from that direction that discovery of Saints John was made. A prospector by the name of J. Coley came over Bear Pass from Breckenridge in 1863 and found silver ore on the crest of Glacier Mountain about a thousand feet up from the town. He smelted his find in a crude furnace with a flue built from a hollow log encased with rocks and clay obtained from the lode for mortar. The outlines are still there.

According to Verna Sharp, Montezuma historian, Coley took his ingots into a bar in Georgetown and showed them around. Promptly other miners came flocking in and made more finds on Glacier Mountain. They called their little settlement Coleyville until a group of Free Masons arrived in 1867. This group altered the name to Saints John, for John the Baptist and John the Evangelist, patron Saints of Masonry.

The camp already had a sober upright character and had welcomed a number of traveling preachers. Prominent among them was Father John L. Dyer, the Methodist minister who is remembered in Colorado for his fine book, *The Snowshoe Itinerant*, as well as for his good works. Father Dyer came by the way of Swan River in 1865 and staked some claims on Glacier Mountain. His route was chosen for the mail between Montezuma and Breckenridge which began tri-weekly service in 1869 and was carried by horseback via Saints John.

In 1872 some of the claims on Glacier Mountain were combined into one property by a company backed with Boston financing. To handle the ore, the Boston company built the best milling and smelting works their Eastern engineers could devise. Later they acquired all the mines on the north side of Glacier Mountain. Their next project was to erect a suitable company town in place of the ramshackle camp. Their plans called for a two-and-a-half story boardinghouse, a company store, an assay office, an ornately trimmed guest house, a mess hall, a foreman's home, a superintendent's home, and residences for the miners. (But oddly there was no school, and the children had to walk to Montezuma.) In 1878 the company town of Saints John was completed.

Unique among mining camps, it boasted that it had no saloon. Instead there was a library of three hundred volumes, donated by Boston friends. Eastern and European newspapers were also sent regularly from the home office. The culture of this pretty, silver town was to be emulated by the gold town of American City—but not its sobriety.

The superintendent lived in town about seven months of the year. During his absence his house was cared for by the manager of the boardinghouse. She permitted a few of the residents to view its wonders. The house was completely furnished with Sheraton furniture, Lenox china, plush draperies, oil paintings, and *objets d'art* on whatnots added the last touch of elegance.

But then came over-production of silver, followed by the silver panic of 1893. The Boston Mining Company shut down, and the superintendent walked out of his home without bothering to lock the door, leaving the furnishings intact. The house was still standing in 1960 but the contents had long since been stolen or vandalized.

The Saints John mine was re-opened and worked in the 1940's and early '50's. But no one lived there. The town of Saints John has been a true ghost town for over half a century, and is unique in our collection for its former decorum, for its being the only company town of the lot, and for its pastoral prettiness.

PRETTY SAINTS JOHN WAS SECLUDED

The superintendent's house was in the best condition of buildings left standing in the former company town. Note fine smelter stack at right.

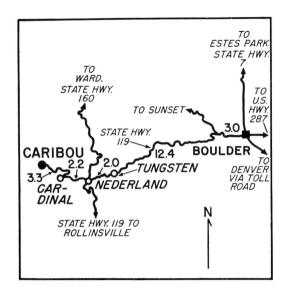

Caribou's fame lives on despite most of its buildings being gone because it had the richest silver mine of the Front Range and because bullion from Caribou formed a $12,000 walkway in April, 1873, for a President. This was at Central City when President U. S. Grant stepped from his stagecoach into the Teller House.

Two mines, the Caribou and the Poor Man, were discovered in August, 1869, by two prospectors working out of Black Hawk. According to historian Don Kemp, they were searching for the location of a float where Samuel P. Conger had picked up a sample of rock. Conger had been on a hunting trip near Arapaho Peak and been attracted by the baffling quality of some unusual boulders.

The two prospectors were lucky. They found the float, staked claims, and set to work during that fall and winter. Their first shipments brought $400 a ton and caused a rush to the area. Many other mines were found, and a city was started—Caribou City. Subsequently, the Caribou mine was sold in two lots for $125,000 to A. D. Breed of Cincinnati. Breed resold the mine and his mill in 1873 to the Nederland Mining Company of Holland for $3,000,000.

Caribou continued until the Silver Panic, and a few residents lingered on into the twentieth century. But after the Caribou mine shut down in 1884, the population fell off. None of the other mines hired such large crews, and gradually they, too, closed. Efforts were made from time to time at re-opening; but because of excessive amounts of underground water, the ventures all failed.

Still, Caribou's silver riches were once glorious and even trod upon by a President!

J. B. Sturtevant, 1887; D.P.L.

WINDY CARIBOU NEARLY BLEW AWAY

In the 1870's and early '80's Caribou grew to a population of nearly five hundred residents. It established law and order, built a Methodist church, opened a school, organized a Cornish band, instituted regular stage service to Central City, and added props to buildings in an effort to withstand the frequent gales. The above ably depicts the wind problem. The lower photo shows Caribou as it looked in 1960 from the same angle on Goat Hill. Arapaho Peak and Baldy are in the background. In the lower photo only the dump (upper left) remained of the famous Caribou mine. The stone foundation (right) and another (too far north to show) were constructed later in an effort to solve the wind problem without props. Whenever old pictures were available, the layout of this booklet endeavors to follow a "then" and "now" presentation.

D.K.P., 1960

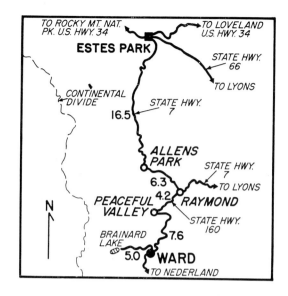

From

Estes

Park

Ward, at an altitude of 9,253 feet, was named for Calvin W. Ward who discovered gold in the vicinity in 1860 after prospecting up Left Hand Creek. From 1865 to '67 when the Ni-Wot and Columbian properties were booming, it had a population of six hundred. (In both pictures on the facing page they may be seen as the two big mines or dumps, high on the mountainside to the left.)

The camp stayed in minor operation during the '70's and '80's and thrived in the late 1890's. It was then that the penniless Horace Tabor, who had been one of the richest men in Colorado, tried to stage a comeback. His fortune had been made in Leadville silver; now he tried Ward gold. He owned a mine called the Eclipse. (The dump may still be seen on the Lodge-of-Pines property.) With a borrowed $15,000 from W. S. Stratton of Cripple Creek, he and Baby Doe set to work, living at the mine. But they were unsuccessful, and it was with relief that during January, 1898, the news reached him in Ward of his appointment as postmaster of Denver.

Six months after Tabor left Ward, a narrow gauge railroad, the Colorado & Northwestern (later D.B.&W.), arrived. It attracted many tourists. An added inducement was that the train stopped long enough to take the stageline to scenic Lake Brainard.

The trains also hauled ore for a while but this business fell off. When the big blizzard of November, 1913, and a cloudburst in July, 1919, damaged the track, abandonment soon followed.

Ward was deserted in the 1920's. But the building of the Peak-to-Peak highway in the late 1930's saved it. The town has survived as a summer resort although its year-around population is only fifteen.

It is unique for having been the scene of Tabor's brave stand.

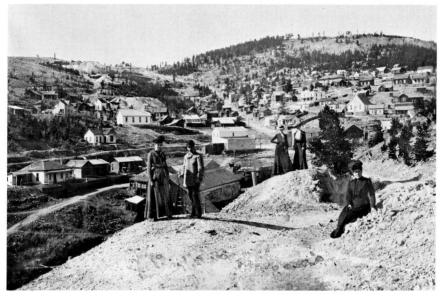

WARD DELIGHTED SUNDAY EXCURSIONISTS

In 1902 Ward had a population of three hundred fifty and advertised that it had six stamp mills in operation as well as good schools and churches. The Columbia Hotel opened that year on the street just below the charming Congregational Church (prominent on the hill). Just above the church on the highest street level was the railroad depot of the Denver, Boulder and Western, now a cafe on the Peak-to-Peak highway.

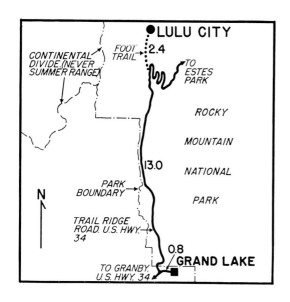

●LULU CITY

CONTINENTAL
DIVIDE (NEVER
SUMMER RANGE)

FOOT
TRAIL

2.4

TO
ESTES
PARK

ROCKY

MOUNTAIN

3.0   NATIONAL

N

PARK
BOUNDARY

PARK

TRAIL RIDGE
ROAD. U.S. HWY.
34

0.8
GRAND LAKE

TO GRANBY.
U.S. HWY. 34

From

Grand

Lake

Lulu City is the first of our ghost towns to carry the inevitable "city" in its formal title. Adding "city" to the name of any little group of four or five log cabins was a habit dear to the hearts of the pioneers who took part in the trans-Mississippi West movement. Filled with optimism, they envisaged any stopping place as a sure metropolis. Witness the number of minute settlements with the imposing adjunct dating even from 1858, the year before the gold rush to Colorado. For example there were Montana City, Denver City, Golden City and Boulder City. Of these the first settlement disappeared completely, and the three survivors dropped the grandiose appendage.

Lulu City, like Montana City, is the disappearing type. In 1960 it was not completely gone, but almost. It was platted in 1879 by Ben F. Burnett who named the town for his oldest daughter. Lulu had only one good year, but hung on until 1883. After that a few die-hard prospectors remained. In the four years of Lulu City's belief that its abundant silver ore would be rich, it had a large hotel, a store, several saloons, homes and a small red-light district. Mixed in with the silver ore found in the mines on the mountainsides to the west, was a little placer gold flecked through the sand of the long meadow. But neither the silver nor the gold were worth much. Lulu City's post office was discontinued in January of 1886.

According to Mary Cairns, whose 1946 book *Grand Lake: The Pioneers* pictured much more of Lulu City than can be seen today, one of the town's prospectors was so discouraged he said:

"Some day you'll see nothing but a foot trail along this street. Raspberry bushes and spruce trees will be growing through the roof of the hotel yonder."

Unknown, 1889; D.P.L.

LULU CITY BECAME A GHOST EVEN BY 1889

Impossible to imagine now: When the town was platted in a park at 9,400 feet altitude, it had one hundred numbered blocks and nineteen streets. The Forest Service and National Parks System have no regard for history and are letting all the nineteenth-century buildings within their boundaries deteriorate as fast as possible. The two high mountains in the background are Lulu and Neota, and the cut is the Grand Ditch.

D.K.P., ,1960

BEAR TRAP

One of the few remaining sights in Lulu City is this unusual device for deluding Mr. Bruin. A piece of meat was set inside. While he was nosing his food, a trip hammer released the door which fell and caged him well.

D.K.P., 1960

His prophecy has come true in full measure—only you can't see the hotel at all! If you count carefully, you can discover the foundations of twenty-three buildings in the main part of town. Some five hundred feet farther north, there is a lone remote ruin in a grove on a point jutting west. This belonged to the town prostitute.

Lulu City's most distinctive relic is at the southern entrance to town—a former bear trap which gives Lulu City its uniqueness today.

The town also had uniqueness in the past. It took part in one of the bloodiest county-seat wars in Colorado history, a war that resulted in the death of four men on July 4, 1883. This carnage was followed by the suicide of a sheriff and the escape of an undersheriff.

Grand County, when created in 1874, was a very large county. Hot Sulphur Springs was the only settlement of any size in the area and was given the county seat. Shortly afterward, gold and silver were found in the mountains which led to the founding of Lulu City, Gaskill and Teller. This mountainous section decided that they should have the county seat and that it should be at Grand Lake. They agitated for an election on the change of county seat and won in 1881.

Many antagonisms and animosities were built up in the course of this contest that kept on festering. Two years later one county com-

30

missioner was allied with the sheriff and deputy sheriff while the two other commissioners were allied with the county clerk. In the midst of a Fourth of July celebration, when the morning was already full of noise of firecrackers and of people sending shots of jubilation out over the lake, a mortal fight began at an ice house near the Fairview Hotel.

By the time people on the hotel porch reached the ice house, two men were dead and two were dying, one of whom claimed he had been attacked by the deputy sheriff. The sheriff and the deputy sheriff fled. The deputy sheriff disappeared, and his end is unproved. Less than three weeks later in a hotel room in Georgetown, the sheriff committed suicide. Mystery still cloaks the cause of the actual shooting.

Although no one of the six was a resident of Lulu City at the time of the tragedy, the undersheriff had been previously, and all the men had been visitors. The dismal affair sounded the death knell of Lulu City.

Not many years afterward the many bears and mountain sheep had the townsite all to themselves, and the bears could laugh at Lulu City's renowned trap.

CHRISTMAS TREES CHOSE CABINS FOR BOXES

A quaint sight and a complete fulfillment of the old prospector's prophecy are these spruce trees growing inside former residences.

D.K.P., 1960

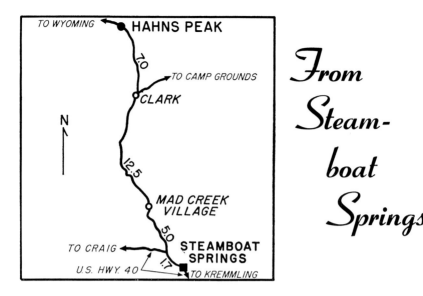

From Steam-boat Springs

Hahns Peak is the lowest in altitude of our selected towns—8,163 feet—and the farthest north—almost to the Wyoming line. It is now solely a summer resort, but a summer resort fully conscious of its mining history. Two monuments fill a grassy plot in its main street.

One is a large hose nozzle which bears a plaque commemorating the work that the "little giant" (as the nozzle was called) did in a former placer operation. The other reads in part: "This monument is dedicated in honor of Joseph Hahn and other pioneers of this great basin. In the summer of 1862, Joseph Hahn, and two unknown companions discovered gold at the foot of this great peak . . ." After the Civil War Hahn returned with two friends who named the peak for Hahn. In the spring of 1867, while Hahn was returning to Empire for supplies, he died in Middle Park of exhaustion.

Most of Hahns Peak's production was placer gold, and close to $1,000,000 was extracted around 1901. Previously in the 1870's the placers were worked with almost no profit because of the cost of building three ditches. There was also a silver-lead mine high on Hahns Peak, the Tom Thumb.

The most amazing bit of the town's history occurred in the winter of 1898 when Hahns Peak (then the seat of Routt County) was the scene of a real "Wild West" TV script. Sheriff Charles Neiman, after a sensational and tricky chase, succeeded in incarcerating two outlaws, Harry Tracy and David Lant, in the Hahns Peak jail. By a ruse they escaped, leaving the sheriff for dead; were recaptured and escaped again. The astounding story is told with full details by Wilson Rockwell in *Sunset Slope* and gives Hahns Peak its unique TV character.

HAHNS PEAK COMMEMORATES ITS FOUNDER

The store at the left is labeled C. E. Blackburn, General Merchandise. Blackburn was in business there during 1902 and '03. In 1904 he was also postmaster. Previously the same building had held the bank. The large building in the center of the photograph (with two windows facing this way) was the Larson Hotel. The three-roofed building was the courthouse. It obscures the jail which stood behind it in 1898, in a direct line with Hahns Peak. On a night that was twenty-eight degrees below zero, Lant and Tracy, outlaws and escapees from the Utah penitentiary, beat and bound the sheriff and left him senseless in the jail. They crossed the street to the livery stable and stole the tired stage team. Courageously captured a second time by the same sheriff, the outlaws escaped again and left Colorado. Details of their story make a thriller. The upper photo was taken by a panoramic camera and makes the main street appear much wider than it really is. It also diminishes the height of Hahns Peak in the background. A number of buildings are identical but appear different because of the two types of cameras. Poverty Bar, the placer and flat which was worked with hydraulic hoses and yielded close to a half million dollars, is off to the left behind the Blackburn Store in the upper photo and the school house in the lower. Herman Mahler, Hahns Peak's oldest resident, worked the placer around 1913. In 1960 he was still faithful to the town for five months of the year. Hahns Peak is completely deserted through the long harsh winter months.

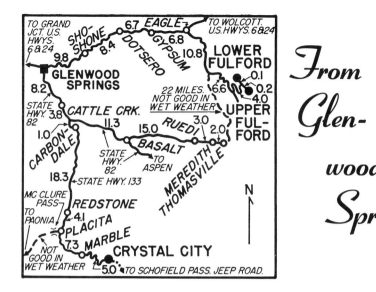

TO GRAND
JCT. U.S.
HWYS.
6&24
SHOSHONE
8.4
6.7 EAGLE
GYPSUM
6.8
DOTSERO
10.8
9.8
GLENWOOD
SPRINGS
8.2
STATE
HWY. 3.8
82
1.0
CARBONDALE
CATTLE CRK.
11.3
15.0
BASALT
STATE
HWY.
82
TO
ASPEN
18.3
STATE HWY. 133
MC CLURE
PASS
TO
PAONIA
REDSTONE
4.1
PLACITA
NOT
GOOD IN
WET WEATHER
7.3 MARBLE
5.0
TO WOLCOTT.
U.S.HWYS. 6&24
LOWER
FULFORD
0.1
0.2
22 MILES.
NOT GOOD IN
WET WEATHER
6.6
4.0
UPPER
FUL-
FORD
RUEDI
3.0
2.0
MEREDITH
THOMASVILLE
N

CRYSTAL CITY
TO SCHOFIELD PASS. JEEP ROAD.

From Glen- wood Springs

Fulford was originally two towns, Camp Nolan and Polar City. They date from the spring of 1887 when prospecting began up East Brush Creek from Eagle. In June of that year William Nolan accidentally shot himself, but his friends continued to call the camp after him because he had been the original leader. It was located on a small slope beside White Quail Creek before it joins Nolan Creek. As rich mines were opened up on New York Mountain, some bearing free gold, Camp Nolan grew until there was no more room.

Newcomers settled farther down in a meadow through which Nolan Creek runs and called the new settlement, Polar City. This name commemorated one of the richest mines on New York Mountain, the Polar Star. Other good producers were the Iron Age, Richmond, and Cave.

Both towns grew side by side until New Year's Eve of 1891. At that time it was the custom of all miners "to take to the hills" on the last day of the year, and 1891 was no exception. Any tenderfoot would immediately ask, "Why?"

The answer lay in the mining laws which stated that any claim, not proved up on by midnight of the fiscal year, was open for relocation. Anyone intrepid enough to get there and drive new stakes could own the property. Miners would eye a good claim enviously and keep tabs to see if the owner was doing the required amount of work. If he was not, woe to him! A new claimant would be driving stakes on his mine while he toasted in the New Year at some saloon.

In 1891 Arthur H. Fulford was a popular resident of Eagle, wellknown there and in Denver. He had mining interests throughout the county and knew of a good property across New York Mountain and

W. Mackey, 1902; Harriette Daggett Collection

FULFORD HAD AN UPPER AND LOWER TOWN

The Lanning Hotel and the Daggett Store may easily be located in both the "then" and "now" shots. In the upper photo New York Mountain (with two elevations) is in the background. White Quail Creek may be seen running down its sides to join Nolan Creek whose banks show in the foreground, this side of Lower Fulford. The road which connected the two towns crosses the hill behind the prominent hotel and store.

D.K.P., 1960

down Bowman Gulch that would be open for re-staking. Accordingly he made an engagement to meet a friend in Camp Nolan the last day of the year so that they could make the difficult hike together.

The two friends greeted each other enthusiastically at the Lanning Hotel (which at that time was in the upper town) and had a sumptuous noon meal. They toasted the New Year and promised themselves great riches from the location they were about to make on the sly. But one hitch developed.

The friend had ordered new skis to be made by hotel-keeper Henry Lanning who was the master craftsman of the camp. As they dined, Lanning informed them that the skis would not be ready until the next day. The friend said he would follow in the morning, bringing supplies for a leisurely return trip, and the two men selected a place to rendezvous. Fulford set out alone.

He was never seen alive again. The next day, when the skis were in good order, the friend followed Fulford's tracks with no difficulty until

UPPER FULFORD HAD A STURDY ASSAY OFFICE

The original assay office (right), just a few steps from White Quail Creek, supported an enormous ridge pole which in turn held a sod roof.

D.K.P., 1960

beyond Bowman Gulch. Then evidence of an enormous snowslide came into view, and the footsteps went no farther. The friend retraced his path and enlisted the help of one hundred men to plumb the depths of the slide. Two days later Fulford's body was found in a sitting position, his eyes still wide open with surprise.

Shaken by the loss, the rescue party determined to rename their towns. From that time on the camps were known as Upper and Lower Fulford. They were incorporated in January, 1896, with a townsite comprising fifty-nine acres. Lower Fulford grew in popularity, and gradually the post office and many businesses moved down to the more roomy location.

Fulford's mines were profitable until about 1903 when the camp died away. The town had another big boom ten years later when one of the prospectors who had stayed on made a new lucky strike. The place was crowded, every empty cabin was appropriated, and the hotel bulged. One mine was named the 1913 Tunnel in honor of its $200-a-ton ore—and then in a few weeks everything fizzled out again.

In 1960 most of its log cabins had been moved down to ranches on Brush Creek. A few old buildings in Lower Fulford had been adapted for hunting and fishing cabins, and the rest were deserted. Upper Fulford was completely ghost. The 1906 wooden bucket for spring water, halfway between the two camps, was still in place, and its water still refreshing.

But the story of Fulford was almost lost. People were more interested in the nearby cave than in the history of the town. Nonetheless the camp seemed unusual in that the names of Fulford and Nolan preserved the memories of two accidents, so typical and so hazardous in the lives of Colorado mining towns—a unique duo . . .

Crystal City, the other ghost town to be reached from Glenwood Springs, is a long, but scenic drive away. The route via the Frying Pan, Roaring Fork and Crystal River Valleys, is especially scenic but to be undertaken with caution (as shown on the map). The ride up the Crystal River, whose bed has been carelessly strewn with great slabs of marble by former cloudbursts, is a fascinating preparation for the special charm of Crystal City. The town lies tucked into a green valley at the forks of the Crystal River and until 1955 could only be reached afoot or on horseback—an isolation helpful to preservation.

On the way up Crystal River the visitor passes through two storied towns that have their own dramatic pasts—Redstone and Marble. Near Marble was the quarry which supplied the white stone for the Lincoln Memorial in Washington, D.C., and the block for the Unknown Soldier's Grave at Arlington, Virginia. A standard gauge railroad, The Crystal River and San Juan, served the town and there connected with

CRYSTAL CITY USED SPARKLING WATER POWER

a four-mile electric line that served the quarry. In many places along the embankment of the river the roadbed has been riprapped with marble, a strange sight. Our ghost town is five miles farther up the Crystal River than the marble finishing plant (now Marble's special ghost).

Crystal City had its beginnings in 1880 when prospectors, working north from Gunnison through Gothic and Schofield, drifted down the south fork of the Crystal River. They found outcroppings of transparent quartz shot with crystallite and called the river and their little settlement, Crystal. From that year until 1885, about seven good silver mines were opened up in the surrounding mountains, notably the Lead King in Lead King Basin, the Inez, the Harrison Farley, the Catalpa, the Sheep Mountain tunnel and the Black Queen.

Isolation was Crystal City's greatest problem. Shipment of ore had to be by long jack trains along treacherous trails either via Schofield to Gothic or down the Crystal River to Carbondale. The trails were harrassed by both rock and snowslides, and the miners who wintered there were completely snowbound. In 1883 a four-mile road was completed from Schofield. Crystal City's population mounted to about three hundred that year and to about four hundred by 1886.

The town had several stores, two newspapers, the *Silver Lance* and the *Crystal River Current*, the usual saloons, two hotels, a barber shop, pool hall and a renowned club—the Crystal Club. It also had a very unusual mill used at different times in its history by the Black Queen, the Sheep Mountain tunnel (which was over half a mile long) and the Lead King. The last time the mill was used was in 1916 when an attempt was made to re-open the first two mines, but the ore was not rich enough for consistent profits.

Crystal City's population fluctuated radically as did that of all mining camps. After the Silver Panic people moved out until in 1915 there were only eight residents. The next year the count rose to over seventy-five because of Black Queen and Sheep Mountain tunnel mining activity. But when this venture failed, Crystal City died completely.

In 1954 Mr. and Mrs. Joseph Neal of Indiana, who were enthralled with the beauty of Crystal City's setting, allied themselves with Mrs. Helen Collins in a movement to preserve the remaining buildings of Crystal City. In 1960 the town was a summer resort, accessible by an automobile road from Carbondale and by a jeep road from Schofield Park and Gunnison County towns.

Its unusual mill stood, if increasingly dilapidated, the most picturesque mill in Colorado, and lent delightful Crystal City a unique charm.

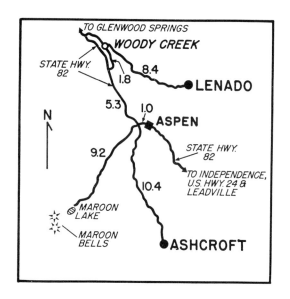

STATE HWY. 82

TO GLENWOOD SPRINGS

WOODY CREEK

8.4

1.8

●LENADO

N

5.3 1.0

ASPEN

9.2

STATE HWY. 82

TO INDEPENDENCE, U.S. HWY. 24 & LEADVILLE

10.4

MAROON LAKE

MAROON BELLS

●ASHCROFT

From

Aspen

The drive to Lenado (which the natives incorrectly call Lenade-o—see over for pronunciation) will take you through a colorful red sandstone area that looks unmineralized. But close to the head and on the south side of Woody Creek were two rich tunnels—the Aspen Contact mine and the Leadville. The unusually rich zinc-lead-silver vein from which they stem was found in the early 1880's by A. J. Varney who climbed out of Aspen up Hunter Creek, over Red Mountain and around the lower reaches of Bald Knob.

Varney formed the Varney Tunnel Company, and a settlement of some three hundred people grew up below the tunnels. They erected log cabins, some frame houses, a store, a boardinghouse, two saloons, a sawmill, a mill for the ore, and a big log barn to shelter the mules used in the mines and for transporting concentrates to Aspen and on to Leadville. The road followed the approximate route Varney had taken when he found the outcropping.

About 1888 the Denver and Rio Grande Railroad (which had arrived in Aspen the year before) graded an eight-mile roadbed up Woody Creek from the Roaring Fork Valley. But later it was decided shipments of ore from Lenado would not support a branch line. Lenado continued operating as it had been until the Panic of '93 when the sawmill, mill and mines shut down. Around the turn of the century they were started up again and ran until 1906.

Then Lenado lapsed to ghost status until 1917 when lead and zinc were needed during World War I. The Smuggler Leasing Company built a new boardinghouse, rebuilt some of the old houses and opened the sawmill and the mines. Trucks were used to transport the ore for milling and smelting elsewhere.

J. E. Spurr, 1898; U.S.G.S.

LENADO BEGAN AS A SILVER CAMP

At the time geologist Spurr took the upper photo he remarked that Lenado was in a rather dilapidated condition, having been badly affected by the Silver Panic. His picture was taken from above the Leadville mine, both higher and farther to the left than the 1960 shot. The latter shows the dump of the Aspen Contact mine, the original old barn for the mine mules and one of the old houses dating from the 1880's.

D.K.P., 1960

LENADO'S NAME MEANS "WOODED"

A busy sawmill has saved the town from death in full prophecy of the unknown man who gave it a Spanish name (pronounced Len-yah-do).

When the need for strategic metals waned, Lenado folded again. In 1935 Jack Flogaus opened up the sawmill to run continuously thereafter. In the summer of 1960 he employed thirty-three men, five of whose families stayed the year round and ten of whose families were summer residents. The cutting of lumber was done on U. S. Forest Service land on Larkspur Mountain and was limited to spruce only.

Lenado is unique because of its sawmill—the only mining camp that was revived from a ghost town by woodcutting . . .

The story of Ashcroft can almost be told by the Colorado Business Directory which listed its population thus: 1881, 200; 1883, 1,000 in summer, winter, uncertain; 1884, 500; 1885, 100; 1890, 50; 1910, 60.

The first prospectors arrived in the summer of 1879 over Pearl Pass, staked some claims and decided to winter at the site of Ashcroft. The town's boom followed in 1882 when Jacob Sands and partners found rich ore in the Montezuma-Tam O'Shanter mines and obtained their financing from Horace Tabor. The town's favorite story is of the big day in the spring of 1883 when the Silver King arrived on an inspection trip with his bride, Baby Doe. A twenty-four hour celebration was held, including a banquet, ball and free drinks at the thirteen saloons.

Ashcroft's fortunes followed the pattern of other small silver camps with minor variations. Its uniqueness today stems from later developments. The Stuart Maces established the most unusual lodge in Colorado there after World War II. They specialized in Toklat Husky dogs, conducting dogsled rides in winter and kennel tours in summer. Toklat Lodge has become internationally famous.

Although the Mace's own building is new, they have tried to foster preservation of the old buildings. In 1960 fifteen of these were still standing, despite the fact that the heavy snows were felling them fast. The Forest Service had established six camp sites nearby with tables and garbage cans but were ignoring everything historical.

Ashcroft is also unique because some of its old buildings were used in filming of the Sergeant Preston TV series, popular about 1956-'57.

(History of the Roaring Fork Valley can be more easily understood if the visitor reads Famous Aspen *and* Glenwood's Early Glamor.*)*

ASHCROFT WAS A BIGGER TOWN THAN ASPEN

Ashcroft had two outlets; one over the passes, Taylor and Cottonwood, to Buena Vista's railhead, the other over Pearl Pass to Crested Butte.

Franz Berko, 1958

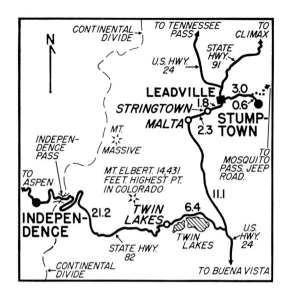

Independence is the town of many names—and yet it never had an official post office of "Independence!"

It happened this way: the camp was started in the spring of 1879 by a group of prospectors from Leadville, headed by Billy Belden. They found an excellent gold placer at the head of the Roaring Fork and settled down to mine. They called the placer and their camp Belden. On the Fourth of July they made another big strike a few yards away and in their jubilation renamed their holdings, Independence, because of the day.

Meanwhile their camp had attracted newcomers who were resented by the first arrivals, and feuds began to flare. The placer claims led to lode discoveries, and by 1880 the Farwell Company of Leadville had secured a dozen of the best properties. They began construction of a mill. At the same time a town promoter, William Kinkead, moved in and changed the name to Chipeta in honor of Chief Ouray's wife. In January, 1881, he secured a postmaster's job for himself with a post office called Sidney.

The Farwell Mining Company disliked Kinkead's action, and six months later they obtained a post office under the name of Farwell. A third group, antagonistic to both the first petitioners, obtained a post office in February, 1882, under the name of Sparkhill. That same year the first two post offices were discontinued, and Sparkhill won. But half the residents still called the settlement Independence.

The town flourished with some four hundred residents until 1887 as both a mining camp and stage-stop on the road between Aspen and Leadville. But when the D. & R. G. and the Colorado Midland railroads arrived in Aspen, people started to move away. In 1888 Independence had a population of one hundred. The remaining residents first changed the name to Mammoth City, then Mount Hope, and then in 1897-'99, during a revival of the mine and mill, back to Chipeta.

After 1900 there was only one resident—the caretaker of the mill, Jack Williams, who called his home, Independence. In 1912 Williams departed, and so died Belden-Independence-Chipeta-Sidney-Farwell-Sparkhill-Mammoth City-Mount Hope-Chipeta-Independence — a town unique in nomenclature . . .

Before sightseeing around Leadville the visitor should read *The Unsinkable Mrs. Brown, Silver Queen, Augusta Tabor* and the *Matchless Mine and Lusty Leadville.* No mining camp in Colorado can equal Leadville for the drama of its history, and it is impossible to catch the region's unique flavor without some preparation beforehand.

There are a number of ghost towns in the environs. The most historic is Oro City in California Gulch, but we have chosen Stumptown because of its association with "The Unsinkable Molly Brown," a musical comedy. To the south are Ball Mountain and fabulous Breece Hill where J. J. Brown was an eighth owner of the Little Jonny.

INDEPENDENCE LIES BESIDE THE HIGHWAY

This, the easiest ghost town to see, is viewable from a parked car and presents a host of interesting shots for the artistic photographer.

Franz Berko, 1957

The Little Jonny was probably Leadville's richest mine. Properties such as the Robert E. Lee made more fantastic shipments—during a seventeen-hour stretch in January, 1880, some $118,500 was extracted—and others such as the Tabors' Matchless have had more publicity. But the Little Jonny was rare in being both a gold and silver mine in a predominantly silver camp.

Its principal owner was John F. Campion ("Leadville Johnny") who employed Jim Brown as a superintendent until Brown was clever enough to find a gold belt in the workings of the mine. This was just at the time that the price of silver was falling and the Panic of 1893 was casting a pall on the silver camps. In return for this stroke of luck the grateful owners cut Brown in for an eighth share of the mine.

Jim Brown had married Maggie Tobin, an illiterate Irish waitress, in 1886. In order to be close to the mines that he was managing at the time, he had taken her to live in Stumptown.

One historian has contended that Stumptown is really Stumpftown, named for Joseph Stumpf. This seems unlikely as Stumpf was reportedly engaged in placering north of Leadville in the lower reaches of Evans Gulch some six miles from Stumptown on the Stumpf placer in the 1890's. In 1897 he obtained the job of hoistman at the Little Jonny mine. At that time, seventeen years after Stumptown's beginnings, Stumpf went to live in Stumptown to be close to his job at the mine. Apparently he lived in the same two-room log cabin (now gone) on the north face of Breece Hill that had been formerly occupied in 1886 by Jim Brown and his bride, Maggie (later "The Unsinkable"). The cabin may very easily have been the property of the Ibex Mining Company, owner of the Little Jonny.

Stumptown began in 1880 with a main street that ran parallel to South Evans Gulch on the west side of the creek. It grew up around the activities of such mines as the Little Bob, St. Louis, Louise, Gold Basin, Winnie, Ollie Reed and Little Ellen (all of which were in South Evans Gulch). Above it on the face of Breece Hill were such famous producers as the Fanny Rawlings, the Big Four, the five shafts of the Little Jonny, the Modoc and the Eclipse.

As "suburbs" of Leadville went, the town was fairly conservative. It was largely residential with a number of saloons, a pool hall and a fine schoolhouse. This building may still be seen in Leadville at the southwest corner of Sixth and Hemlock Streets where it was moved to serve as the Union Hall.

Stumptown has only two dwellings left and is a complete ghost town, but unique because of "The Unsinkable," an Irish lass who survived the sinking of the *Titanic*.

46

THE "UNSINKABLE" MRS. BROWN LIVED HERE

Stumptown lies in South Evans Gulch, east of Leadville. It was the place where Maggie Tobin Brown lived as the bride of Jim Brown, manager of the Little Jonny mine. It is also where she is supposed to have lost a fortune by hiding paper money in a stove and having it burned. The upper photo looks west toward the Sawatch Range past the Ollie Reed mine; the lower, toward Mosquito Pass and the burro race trail.

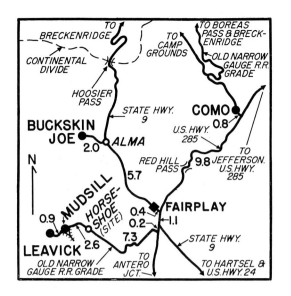

From Fair-play

Buckskin Joe and Leavick are the principal trips here although Como and Mudsill are circled on the map because of photos (over). Buckskin Joe was a famous placer camp discovered in August, 1859, by eight prospectors led by Joseph Higganbottom. Since he was a mountaineer who habitually wore clothes of tanned deer skin, his nickname was "Buckskin Joe." The diggings were named after him.

The town flourished under this name and Lauret for most of the 1860's, having in 1861 a population of five or six hundred including twenty or thirty women. At least half the residents made their living from saloons, hotels, gambling dens and variety halls which caused Buckskin Joe to be described in the *Rocky Mountain News* as South Park's "liveliest little burg." By 1874 its population had dropped to fifty, and several years later it was dead. Its creation of the Silverheels legend makes it unique, and people say her cabin still stands in the trees across the creek . . .

Leavick is unique because it existed sixteen years as a settlement without a name. From 1880 to 1896 there was a group of miners, sometimes as high as two hundred, living in the shadow of Horseshoe Mountain (see photos) close to the Last Chance and Hilltop mines and their mill. The settlement had two saloons, stores, a house of ill repute, and no name.

Finally when the narrow gauge railroad arrived in 1896, the town was named after Felix Leavick, prominent mining man of Leadville and Denver, who owned properties in the Mosquito Range. Leavick had a sporadic life until 1910 with occasional fake bursts after that. Today most of its buildings have been moved to South Park City, a tourist town on the edge of Fairplay.

George Wakely, 1864; C.H.S.

DID "SILVERHEELS" DANCE HERE IN THE 1860'S?

Buckskin Joe was the mining camp that created one of the most delightful Colorado legends. Silverheels was a beautiful dancehall girl who stayed to nurse the miners during a smallpox epidemic after all the other women fled. Later, when the miners raised a purse to reward her, she could not be found. Smallpox had attacked and ravaged her beauty; so she disappeared. In memory, Mount Silverheels was named for her.

D.K.P., 1960

D.K.P., 1960

RAILROAD GHOSTS HAUNT SOUTH PARK

At Mudsill the wye of the Denver, South Park and Hilltop narrow gauge is all that remains of a small camp created by the activities of the Mudsill mine. Below is the sad, abandoned D.S.P. & P. roundhouse at Como.

Michael Davis, 1960

THE PARK'S MINING GHOSTS ARE MANY

The Leavick terminus of the Last Chance and Hilltop mines' tramway was at the above mill. Ore buckets swung in the second story (right), emptied and back along the towers. Below is an arastra in Buckskin Creek.

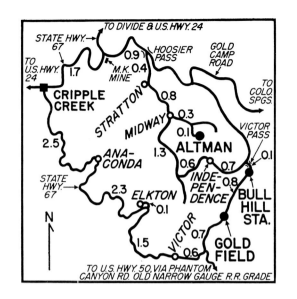

From

Cripple

Creek

Next to Leadville, the Cripple Creek district has the most fascination for the preterist. It had the most fabulous gold production of any camp in Colorado—nay, in the United States. According to historian Marshall Sprague, the district created twenty-eight millionaires as a modest estimate. One of those who made a million was lumberman Sam Altman. Formerly he ran a sawmill in Poverty Gulch but in 1893 he founded a town, Altman.

His town was close to three big producers, the Pharmacist, Victor and Buena Vista, and to his own mine, the Free Coinage on Bull Hill. By November of 1893, the town was supporting four restaurants, six saloons, six groceries, several boardinghouses and a telephone. A schoolhouse and two hundred frame or log houses had been erected, and the loyal citizens claimed a population of twelve hundred.

From its high perch Altman could look down on Independence, Goldfield, Cameron and many another mushrooming settlement that burgeoned in the Cripple Creek excitement of the early '90's. It was not a dressy camp, but a workaday place peopled solely by miners. These miners were workers—hard workers—and they thought they should be more justly rewarded for their labor.

One of Altman's miners was John Calderwood, a Scotsman and a graduate of the McKeesport School of Mines in the class of 1876. He elected to be an organizer for the Western Federation of Miners, a newly formed union born in Butte, Montana, in May, 1893. He was no firebrand but a dignified conscientious worker. Within two months he had signed up every Altman miner for his Free Coinage Union No. 19, W. F. M., and promised them a standard eight-hour three-dollar day.

T. H. Routh, 1894; D.P.L.

ALTMAN CLAIMED TO BE THE HIGHEST TOWN

Altman was platted by Sam Altman in 1893 on the short saddle between Bull Hill and Bull Cliff and soon had a population of fifteen hundred (including Midway a hamlet to the northwest). Its altitude was 10,620 feet. It claimed to be the highest incorporated town in the world and probably was, in North America. Both upper and lower shots were taken near the crest of Bull Hill with Pikes Peak looming in the background. Bull Hill was the scene of one of the early skirmishes of labor-capital battles and was notable as the first significant victory for labor. Part of the maneuvering was comic opera and part, raw violence.

The mine owners were enraged at his demand. In February, 1894, twelve of them banded together in an agreement that their mines would operate solely on a nine-hour three-dollar day. One of the signers was Sam Altman who sat back to see what the residents of his town would do next.

Under Calderwood's bidding five hundred men walked out of the nine-hour mines. Bull Hill, practically in Altman's back yard, was one of the areas most affected because a number of nine-hour mines were located there.

Calderwood organized a central kitchen at Altman to feed the out-of-work miners. He collected funds, trained pickets, assessed the working miners and addressed daily meetings. By March the Bull Hill mine owners were no longer scoffing. Winfield Scott Stratton, richest operator in the district, sent for Calderwood and offered a compromise of $3.25 for a nine-hour shift by day and the same wages for an eight-hour shift by night.

Calderwood accepted the compromise and signed a contract. A contract with a union leader was an unheard of thing in that day and stirred the whole state into editorials and epithets. It made the mine owners of Bull Hill bull-headed, and they attempted force to re-open their mines. But Calderwood made a fortress out of Altman.

He kept order but he also kept anything in the way of a scab or a mine owner out. The mine owners appealed to Governor Waite for militia which arrived and was withdrawn, leaving Calderwood in possession of Altman and Bull Hill. Unfortunately, Calderwood decided to tour the state on behalf of the miners' cause. Without his calm wise leadership the criminal element drifted in and violence took over.

The final peace treaty was signed at Altman on June 10, 1894, after one hundred and thirty days of the strike—the longest in American history up to that time. The nine-hour mine owners gave in on the question of an eight-hour day.

The Battle of Bull Hill was over, and Altman went back to the business of mining. Later on it was the hang-out for the Jack Smith gang and saw some shootings. But mostly the town just mined until the second Cripple Creek strike occurred a decade after the first.

It maintained a steady population until that time. But after the ill effects of the second strike, mines shut down and miners moved out. In 1910 its population had dropped to one hundred. After that it fell off consistently until there was no one.

Altman is unique in our collection—and in the United States—as the scene of the first major strike war and of the first workers' victory—a truly unique presage of the twentieth century.

THE CRIPPLE CREEK DISTRICT HAS MORE GHOSTS

Goldfield was platted in January, 1895, and had a population of thirty-five hundred. It served rather as a suburb to Victor but did build a few substantial buildings, including this fire house. Its quaint engine has been removed to Victor for display. The Bull Hill station (below) is a reminder of three railroads that formerly served Cripple Creek and also of the Independence station blown up by Harry Orchard, 1904.

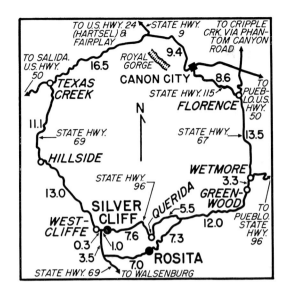

TO U.S. HWY. 24 — STATE HWY. 9 — TO CRIPPLE CRK. VIA PHANTOM CANYON ROAD
(HARTSEL) & FAIRPLAY
TO SALIDA. U.S. HWY. 50 — 16.5 — ROYAL GORGE — 9.4
TEXAS CREEK
CANON CITY — 8.6
STATE HWY. 115 — TO PUEBLO. U.S. HWY. 50
FLORENCE
N
11.1
STATE HWY. 69
STATE HWY. 67 — 13.5
HILLSIDE
STATE HWY. 96 — 7
WETMORE — 3.3
13.0
QUERIDA
GREENWOOD
SILVER CLIFF — 5.5
12.0 — TO PUEBLO. STATE HWY. 96
WEST-CLIFFE
7.6
0.3 — 1.0
7.3
3.5
7.0 — ROSITA
STATE HWY. 69 — TO WALSENBURG

From Canon City

Two interesting mountain spots may be seen in this locality. Rosita, which dates from 1873, is a true ghost town with no one living there in 1960 save the postmistress. But Silver Cliff is no ghost, despite the fact that it was for a decade or more from 1910 on. Both are former county seats of Custer County, and both lost the honor as their silver mines gave out.

Silver Cliff is five years younger than Rosita and experienced a much greater boom than any other mining camp in Colorado with the exception of Leadville. Its first shipment of ore from the gargantuan and unique silver cliff (site of both photos) was in 1878. The population rose to some fifteen thousand in 1881 at the peak of its three-year rush. The Denver and Rio Grande Railroad reached there in May, 1881, and was welcomed with celebration.

Its fire department, established in 1879 in the Town Hall (the lonely building facing this way in the 1960 shot, and now a museum), soon distinguished itself as a frequent winner in the state tournaments of hose cart races for volunteer firemen . . .

Rosita (which means "Little Rose" in Spanish) was the principal town in the Wet Mountain Valley for five years before Silver Cliff and Westcliff (now the county seat) usurped its priority. It had the honor of being the subject of an article written by Helen Hunt Jackson and published in *Scribners Monthly* for May, 1878. The author ("H. H.") claimed there were three hundred mines at the time—but she probably did not know a mine from a prospect hole. She stayed at an inn called *The House of the Snowy Range*, and her descriptions made Rosita and its setting sound as poetically unique as its name.

W. Cross, circa 1890; U.S.G.S.

ROSITA'S HANDSOMEST HOUSE LIVED ON

In the 1890 photo the ornate two-story house (seen below) stood at the righthand end of the main street, facing this way. In 1960 the house next was gone except for some lumber on the ground; the third house still stood. The mansion bore a sign Post Office which was tacked up in 1957 during the filming of Saddle the Wind, *a movie that starred Robert Taylor and used Rosita for atmosphere. Both are now gone.*

D.K.P., 1960

L. C. McClure, 1900-1909; D.P.L.

SILVER CLIFF CHOSE A MAGNIFICENT BACKDROP

Silver Cliff boomed in 1879 to such an extent that it rivaled Leadville for a decade. For a short period it was the third largest town in Colorado and it has never been a true ghost town, although much fallen from its former opulence. What has never changed is the view from the silver cliff, facing the town, across the Wet Mountain Valley to the spectacular reddish Sangre de Cristo Range (Blood of Christ in Spanish).

D.K.P., 1960

From

Salida

Turret was a gold camp that was discovered very late—in 1897—and experienced a boom the following spring. It was located on the south side of Nipple Mountain (which is a spur of Turret Mountain) in a valley at the head of Cat Gulch. The _Rocky Mountain News_ for May 14, 1898, carried a long article describing the excitement in "Turret City" and the possibilities of the various lodes.

Houses were going up fast, and lots were in great demand. Stores, an assay office and saloons were doing business, and a hotel was planned. A post office was open, and daily mail was arriving from Salida. 'The article was exuberant at the gold showing in hematite, jasper and schist and spoke of the Monterrey lode as having great promise.

The town's population, after the usual boomers and drifters departed, was around three or four hundred. In 1900 the _Denver Republican_ ran an article devoted largely to Turret's mines and spoke of the mineralization being in the "Salida Copper Belt" and of the Gold Bug mine's fine shipments of ore. The town was prospering.

By 1907 the population had slipped to two hundred fifty. Still it hung on with a steady flow of gold, gradually lessening to a trickle, until 1939 when there were but twenty-six residents. In 1941 the post office was discontinued, and finally Turret died.

Steve Frazee, prolific Colorado author, two of whose books have become films (_Gold of the Seven Saints_ and _Many Rivers to Cross_) and whose 1961 offering was _More Damn Tourists_, has this provocative recollection:

"When I went to Turret in 1932 to operate a mine, there were thirty-seven inhabitants, three of whom were old timers, since they had

N. W. Meigs, 1902; Virgil Jackson Collection

TURRET FACED THE COLLEGIATE RANGE

The cliffs which gave Turret its name are to the rear of the photographer in both shots. These photos look across the Arkansas Valley to Shavano and Antero Peaks. When the 1902 picture was taken, Turret had a population of one hundred ninety-five and was reached by stage from Salida. Note the residences on the hill at the far end of the main street where the 1960 shot caught a sod roof and amateur chimney.

D.K.P., 1960

been there from the 1890's. One, Pete G. Schlosser of Illinois, claimed to be the first man to eat tomatoes and thus prove they were non-poisonous. Another, Emil Becker of Pittsburgh, Pennsylvania, had been the most active prospector of all, discovering mines and selling them. He was a former big league ball player, having pitched to Connie Mack. One of his old teammates, Billy Sunday, visited Becker when the latter was running a saloon in Turret, and that is a story in itself."

In 1960 Turret had fifteen houses standing. The largest (which may have been the Gregory Hotel) was painted white, cared for, and evidently inhabited as a summer home. Two or three others appeared also to have been redeemed from the mountain rats by weekend sojourners. But the remainder were true ghosts.

Turret has a stimulating view of Shavano and Antero Peaks and the Collegiate Range. It is unique for the castle-like cliffs which stand guard to the east and which gave the town its name . . .

Bonanza, or Bonanza City, dates from early in 1880 when gold was found along Kerber Creek. An episode occurred about the naming of Bonanza which is probably unique in the annals of Colorado. The city fathers decided on Bonanza City as a name. In consequence the town was so incorporated in December, 1880, but they changed their minds. One month later, in January, 1881, the town was re-incorporated as Bonanza. This has led to considerable confusion during the years—some historians claiming that Bonanza is one of Colorado's seven incorporated "cities"—which it is not.

The town's boom began in the summer of 1880 when there was a rush to Kerber Creek. Four towns sprang up of which Bonanza is the sole survivor. For a few it had a population of some fifteen hundred while thirty-two businesses tended to Bonanza's needs. But the district's ore was a disappointment—far from bonanza. It proved to be low grade and also refractory. In the mid-1880's the town almost died.

Then Mark Beidell imported new machinery for the Michigan mine and mill and proved that the ore values could be recovered for small but adequate profit. Slowly others emulated this example, and by 1900 the Bonanza, Exchequer and Eagle mines had been re-opened. More mines such as the Wheel of Fortune, St. Joe and K. O. also produced steadily. The ores were largely lead, zinc and silver with a little copper.

Bonanza has never died. In 1910 it had a population of one hundred. Some thirty people were still living there the year around in 1960, the men actively mining and hoping for the price of metals to rise. Many buildings were standing, at least half of them deserted.

Bonanza is unique in our collection because of the anomaly of its name—a real misnomer.

BONANZA

Bonanza City was actually no bonanza. It had many mines and quantities of low-grade ore which supplied some good fortunes but no millions. It spread for over a mile along Kerber Creek and absorbed an early rival, Kerber City.

Charles Goodman, mid-1880's; D.P.L.

KERBER CREEK IGNORES THE GLORIOUS PAST

The 1960 shot was at the upper end of Bonanza and depicts the farthest house in town, opposite a well and the Wheel of Fortune mine dump.

D.K.P., 1960

From Buena Vista

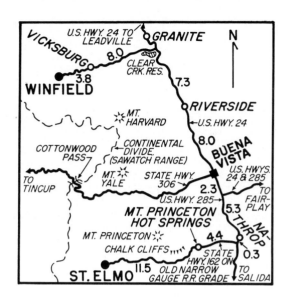

A drive up Chalk Creek around the south side of Mt. Princeton and past the Chalk Cliffs (as famed in their way as those of Dover) will bring you to St. Elmo. This mining camp was located first as Forest City in December, 1880, but shortly after received a post office under the name of St. Elmo. Its main reason for existence was the Mary Murphy mine which had been located five years before and was sold in 1880 to a St. Louis company. There were other gold and silver mines in the locality, such as the Brittenstein group, but many did not warrant the capital expended.

St. Elmo's second reason for existence was the arrival of the narrow gauge, Denver, South Park and Pacific Railroad, which was building toward Gunnison. The grade required a tunnel under the continental divide, west of St. Elmo. In the face of howling blizzards and much labor trouble, work on the Alpine Tunnel went on while St. Elmo acted as a supply depot. The tunnel was completed the following year in December, 1881, and regular service through the tunnel commenced in the summer of '82. According to the Colorado Business Directory, St. Elmo's population was three hundred in these years but dropped to two hundred and fifty when some of the mines proved to be mirages.

But the Mary Murphy held up through the years, employing around one hundred men. According to Louisa Ward Arps (Chalk Creek historian), its peak year was 1914 when a crew of two hundred and fifty was hired. The mine had a tramway nearly 5000 feet long which ran down Pomeroy Mountain from the tunnel outlet at the fourth level to the railroad grade in the gulch. The Mary Murphy finally ceased operation in the 1920's with a total production of around $14,000,000.

Unknown, 1884-90; D.P.L.

SAINT ELMO HAD A CLIFTON HOTEL

The upper view shows one of the two main blocks that was destroyed by fire in 1890. The Clifton Hotel was the large white building in the center of the upper view. The white building at the right was a saloon—note bartenders with white aprons and man holding a beer keg. In the original picture, the stage road to Tin Cup Pass can just be discerned, wending its way up through the timber at far left.

D.K.P., 1960

During its heyday St. Elmo was a little hub, having in addition to its railroad, toll roads west to Tin Cup, north to Aspen and south to Maysville. Accordingly it was a favorite spot with the miners for Saturday night celebrations. But when trips through the tunnel stopped in 1910, and trains up Chalk Creek were halted in 1926, St. Elmo was doomed. Finally there were only two residents of St. Elmo, Annabelle Stark and her brother, Tony, who were to be the subject of many articles. Until their deaths, each one's mounting eccentricities made them legendary, and St. Elmo unique . . .

Winfield started in 1880 and had a post office, one store, two hotels, two saloons and enough cabins to make a population of around thirty. By 1883 it had a number of mines operating which were shipping their silver and copper ore to Leadville for smelting. One of these mines was the Augusta, owned by Jacob Sands (the lover of Baby Doe who brought the beautiful Colorado divorcee to Leadville). Jake was a friend of Horace Tabor's and eventually lost his sweetheart to the Silver King (as Tabor was called). But what made Jake name his mine after Tabor's first wife? Probably Tabor gave him some money for development since the claim was located on May, 10, 1880, several weeks before Tabor and Baby Doe met. The mine is a long crosscut tunnel in Hummel Basin about two miles northwest of Winfield. The Augusta made money for a while but produced no fortune.

Still, the strange puzzle of the mine's name and hidden history does give Winfield a unique quality.

WINFIELD

The Clear Creek district of Chaffee County had seven mining camps rivaling each other in 1881. Only two survived, Vicksburg and Winfield. Today both have been changed into summer resorts where fishing is the principal sport and main attraction.

D.K.P., 1960

Tin Cup was "a wild 'un." Probably Creede, Leadville and Tin Cup attained the worst reputations (and rightfully) of Colorado's many mining camps. Tin Cup was particularly hard on marshals. The first two officeholders were weak and completely under control of the vice element who ran the gambling dens, sporting houses and saloons full tilt. The marshals' orders were to give an appearance of law and order so as to make it easier to fleece the suckers.

Finally conditions grew so bad that a sincere attempt was made to straighten up the corruption. The first strong marshal, Harry Rivers, was shot in a gun battle. His successors were shot, resigned, went insane, or got religion and changed their calling to that of the pulpit. Their infamous story has been very ably portrayed by Rene Coquoz, Leadville historian. "Frenchie," the saloon keeper who shot one of the marshals, ran a place across from the Town Hall at Washington and Grand Streets. The saloon still stands.

Tin Cup's history begins very early in 1861. A prospecting party that consisted of Jim Taylor and two companions was camped on the Taylor River. One of the men brought back to camp some promising looking gravel in a tin cup which suggested the idea of a name for the region. They did a little placering; but in the next years the Civil War curtailed mining activities throughout Colorado. Nothing much happened in the region until the late 1870's when strikes were made on the Gold Cup, the Tin Cup, the Anna Dedricka and the Jimmy Mack. Immediately there was a rush to the area, and in 1879 the town of Virginia City was surveyed and platted.

Frank Hall, one of Colorado's most eminent historians, says in Volume IV of his comprehensive work that the surface ores were high

66

Unknown, 1906; D.P.L.

TIN CUP'S TOWN HALL LOOKS CHURCHLY

During Tin Cup's revival a Town Hall was erected in 1906 and used for a variety of community affairs. The Town Hall was renovated and re-painted in 1950 by the Civic Association. Tin Cup had no church.

Bryant McFadden, 1960

grade silver, ranging from 114 to 600 ounces of silver per ton, and that all had admixtures of gold. In addition there were some excellent placers and gold lodes. In 1880 the Gold Cup mine sold for $300,000, and the town was firmly on its way.

By 1881 when George Crofutt wrote his *Grip-Sack Guide of Colorado* he reported that Virginia City had changed its name to Tin Cup to conform with the name of the region. He added that Tin Cup was a prosperous mining town of six hundred population with twelve stores, several hostels and one smelter. (He omitted the more flagrant business emporiums.) He stressed that game was very abundant and gave the fare for the daily line of sleighs running to St. Elmo.

The Colorado Business directory puts the population figure for 1881 at five hundred, a hundred less than Crofutt. It is interesting to note on this matter of population that present-day writers have a habit of enlarging the figures enormously, especially so-called historians of ghost towns who generally add a zero to any number they encounter. If Colorado's hundreds of mining camps had as many people living in them as is claimed by post-World War II writers, the state would have been as populous then as it is now. But it was not.

Tin Cup, despite the fact that it has had enormous publicity through Pete Smythe's radio and TV show of the same name and through the building of an amusement park west of Denver called East Tin Cup, must be seen in the same light. It was just another mining town, although colorful in its own way, and by the late 1880's was very much in decline.

In 1891 it had a revival and kept going fairly well through that decade. It picked up even more after the turn of the century when the gold mines put on larger crews and when dredging machinery was moved in to operate the placers. But following the usual pattern of these towns, World War I ushered in a growing paralysis, and by 1917 the Gold Cup mine, Tin Cup's mainstay, shut down.

Tin Cup slumbered on in a complete trance except for an occasional sportsman. Little by little its quaint charm, including fire hydrants that date from 1891, attracted more people. By 1960 it was a substantial summer resort with more people taking over the many deserted cabins and buildings and telling of its unique wild past . . .

Gothic is reached by returning down the Taylor River to Almont and taking the road up the East River to its junction with Copper Creek. Crofutt described it in 1881 as the most important mining camp in Gunnison County with a population of nine hundred and fifty. It was established June 8, 1879, and made rapid progress, having many large stores, hotels, restaurants, saloons, shops of all kinds, a public school, a smelter (which Frank Hall says never operated), three sawmills and a weekly newspaper. Shortly its population rose to fifteen hundred.

But, as one old-timer recalled, the Gothic district was the paradise of prospectors but not of miners. It was streaked on every mountainside with protruding veins of quartz. A blind man could locate a claim. But the ore values were not high enough for exploitation. The district had only its unusual beauty amid its surrounding peaks—Treasury, Cinnamon, Galena, Baldy, Belleview and Italian—and to the north the towering Elk Mountains.

Gothic died. Only one resident remained until Dr. John C. Johnson, a former dean at the Western State College in Gunnison, saw its possibilities in 1928 for a fully accredited six-weeks summer school—the Rocky Mountain Biological Laboratory—and bought the two-hundred-acre town. Each year its distinguished staff of scientists invites other eminent scholars in the biological field to a conference and symposium at the end of the regular teaching session. Such topics as "The Living Balance Between Flora and Fauna" are discussed. The laboratory has brought Gothic into a national prominence never attained by its mines.

The Rocky Mountain Biological Laboratory with its nine hundred and five acres of primitive spruce and fir land, which sweep up the side of Baldy Mountain, made Gothic unique in 1960. It was the only ghost town that had turned into a school.

GOTHIC HAS TURNED FROM MINES TO PLANTS

Garwood Judd, variously known as "The Man Who Stayed" and "Mayor of Gothic," lived off and on in the Town Hall until his death in 1930.

Bryant McFadden, 1958

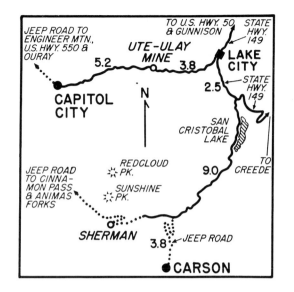

Map labels:

JEEP ROAD TO ENGINEER MTN., U.S. HWY. 550 & OURAY

TO U.S. HWY. 50 & GUNNISON

STATE HWY. 149

UTE-ULAY MINE

5.2   3.8

LAKE CITY

2.5

STATE HWY. 149

CAPITOL CITY   N

SAN CRISTOBAL LAKE

TO CREEDE

JEEP ROAD TO CINNAMON PASS & ANIMAS FORKS

REDCLOUD PK.

SUNSHINE PK.

9.0

SHERMAN   3.8   JEEP ROAD

● CARSON

From Lake City

Capitol City is unique for two reasons—the odd spelling of its name and the sad ruin of one man's dream to have his town the capital of Colorado. He was George S. Lee, a mill and smelter operator.

Frank Fossett wrote in 1880 in his *Colorado* that Capitol City was located at the junction of the two forks of Henson Creek, nine miles west of Lake City, in a park most of which was embraced by the Lee townsite patent. The park was surrounded by rugged, towering San Juan peaks, rich in silver, lead and iron ores. Two smelters were in operation at each end of town. Fossett added:

"Right here . . . where one would least expect to find it is the most elegantly furnished house in Southern Colorado. The handsome brick residence of George S. Lee and lady, distinguished for their hospitality, is a landmark of this locality."

George Lee suffered from the same disease that characterized so many of the pioneers—a compound of boundless optimism and grandiose ambition. He pictured his remote town as the capital of the state and his home as the governor's mansion. Perhaps it was an idea spoken in jest; perhaps it was his sincere dream. Folklore leans to the latter version—but he never campaigned for his idea nor introduced any bill into the legislature.

The name of his town is equally confusing. After Lake City was started in 1874 and platted in 1875, prospectors streamed up Henson Creek, and a town was built at its forks. The newspapers of 1876 and '77 referred to the town as Capital City, and the Colorado Business Directory for the late 1870's used interchangeably the two spellings of *Capital* and *Capitol*. Yet in 1961 the Postmaster General's office in

Washington wrote that "a search of the records for 1876 and '77 reveals that the spelling of the town referred to was Capitol City." To confuse matters still further the Colorado State Archives office has recorded a communication, dated May 2, 1887, from the county commissioners of Hinsdale County in which they petition for permission to change the name of Galena City to Capitol City.

Why is this petition eleven years late? Poor Capitol City—the whole situation seems as confused as George Lee's dream! And who was it did not know that "capitol" is a building, not a town?

According to the historians, Jean and Don Griswold, Capitol City had two prosperous periods when mining and smelting were booming—a silver boom in the mid-1880's and a gold boom around the turn of the century. Two factors prevented Capitol City from attaining any major growth. Early litigation discouraged and slowed up the first business activity of the late 1870's and early 1880's, and later the gold deposits of the 1900's were not very large. The population of around three hundred in 1880 became discouraged and drifted away. In 1885 there were but one hundred people residing there, and in 1900 there was the same number again.

In 1960 there were not many remaining signs of human habitation in Capitol City. Above the junction of North Henson Creek with Henson Creek there were some log cabins in what used to be the upper end of town. On the townsite proper there was only the derelict mansion which was being destroyed from every angle. Henson Creek had altered its course and was eating away the embankment on which the Lee house stood while at the same time human hands were carting away souvenirs. At the lower end of town only the foundations could be seen of the smelter on which George Lee had based his great dream . . .

Continuing up Henson Creek in the direction that the stagecoach used to travel from Lake City to Ouray, the visitor will come to the ruins of Rose's Cabin. Henson Creek was named for Henry Henson who prospected the valley in 1871 prior to the Brunot Treaty of 1873 which took the land away from the Utes. Rose's Cabin was named for Corydon Rose who built it in 1874. It was a hotel and bar with outlying stables and shed and served as a welcome stage stop on the hard ride over Engineer Pass, the most spectacular pass in Colorado, the road now altered to another ridge to make a popular jeep ride . . .

Returning to Lake City the visitor will pass the Ute and Ulay mine. At one time this was such a large operation that a town grew up around its workings. The mill is disused and defunct, and the dam which supplied its water power is broken. But the superintendent's house is occupied by a caretaker who guards the property summer and winter.

From "Colorado" by Frank Fossett, 1880; D.P.L.

THE GRANDEUR OF CAPITOL CITY IS DUST

The elaborate layout of George S. Lee was depicted in Frank Fossett's 1880 publication. The outlying barns, pastures and corrals are now gone. It is evident from this sketch that the course of Henson Creek must have been at the southern limit of Capitol Park. Today Henson Creek is flowing so close to the mansion that it is about to undermine the foundation. The 1960 view looks up the valley toward Rose's Cabin.

D.K.P., 1960

The Ute-Ulay is now part of the holdings of the powerful Newmont Mining Company which also owns the Idarado Mining Company of Ouray and Telluride and the Resurrection Mining Company of Leadville. There is always the off chance that the price of metals will rise, and, should this be the case, many a Colorado mining property would throw off its ghostly pall and throb again with activity . . .

From Lake City a number of ghost towns can be seen but the most exciting one requires a jeep. This is Carson which during the years of its history was also known as Carson Camp and Carson City. Since Carson City's population during the score or so years of its existence from the 1880's to the early 1900's was at no time more than fifty and generally around twenty, one is inevitably reminded by Bayard Taylor's words:

"I only wish that the vulgar snobbish custom of attaching 'city' to every place of more than three houses, could be stopped. From Illinois to California it has become a general nuisance, telling only of swagger and want of taste and not of growth."

Bayard Taylor wrote these words in 1866. The "city" that called forth his ire was Gate City, or Golden Gate City, a string of four or five cabins, at the mouth of Tucker Creek on the stagecoach road to Central City. He included these words the next year in his book *Colorado: A Summer Trip,* and I first quoted the passage in my 1943 Master's Thesis about Central City for the University of Denver. In 1960 when I was re-visiting many ghost towns; I thought of Bayard Taylor's wish frequently and smiled because Taylor never attained his wish. The vogue of adding "city" to the name of any little hamlet continued unabated through the whole nineteenth century and even into the twentieth.

Carson, or Carson City, deserved its appendage more than some at the time of its naming and particularly deserves it today. Of all the towns in our 1960 selection it gave the greatest feeling of being a ghost town. Its buildings have been preserved by the cold and by the fortunate fact that it is in an unusual spot which is not subject to snowslides. This aspect is very rare in the San Juans where thundering snow is man's greatest enemy.

J. E. Carson discovered a mine in 1881 on top of the continental divide some sixteen miles southwest of Lake City on the headwaters of Wager Creek. He staked claims on both sides of the divide, the claims on the south side being at the head of Lost Trail Creek which flows south into the Rio Grande River. With the arrival of other prospectors the Carson Mining district was organized, and in 1882 a camp started. The Griswolds in their *Colorado's Century of Cities* have remarked that Carson was thrown like a cavalry saddle across the continental divide

with one stirrup hanging on the Atlantic slope and one on the Pacific—
a most apt description.

The construction of both segments of Carson is very good—all
the buildings are nicely shingled and show care in their carpentry. But
the Atlantic slope, or higher, section of Carson is in much greater dis-
repair and will not survive very long.

In the '80's Carson mined silver, and after the Panic of 1893
the camp mined gold. But the problem of transportation to a town which
lay at various levels from 11,500 feet to 12,360 was almost insoluble.
Its ore was gold, ruby silver and copper, running sometimes as high as
$2,000 a ton. Despite the richness of the ore the deposits ran in pockets,
occasionally as high as $40,000 in a pocket of only forty feet depth.
But when a pocket was stoped out, then the ore was completely gone.
Among the best mines were the Maid of Carson, Big Injun, Saint Jacob,
Dunderberg and Lost Trail.

And today Carson, although it is unique in its preservation, is a
place where riches are indeed a lost trail!

CARSON SNUGGLES AGAINST THE DIVIDE

*This section of the town lies on the Pacific slope side of the divide
and is in much better condition than the camp on the Atlantic side.*

D.K.P., 1960

From Creede

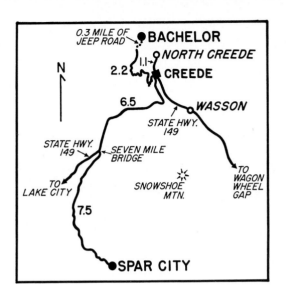

Bachelor's beginnings followed the silver rush to the Creede area in the autumn of 1890. The town was heralded by an amusing paragraph in the *Creede Candle* for January 21, 1892, which ran:

"The latest townsite excitement is in a park on Bachelor Hill, around the Last Chance boarding house. Two saloons and a female seminary are already in operation and other business houses are expected soon. It is to be called Bachelor."

By April the 10,500-foot-high town had a post office (Teller, because of a conflict with Bachelor, California), a theatre, eight stores, a dozen saloons and several boardinghouses, restaurants and hotels. A number of two-story buildings were being erected. By June the town had been incorporated and was holding an election of officers. By December it had a new opera house which was packed when the Bachelor City Dramatic Club presented the drama *Wild Irishman*, interspersed with several divertissements and followed by a dance, in an effort to raise money for a Catholic church.

But the efforts of the better people failed. The character of Bachelor remained tough. At the height of its population of around twelve hundred, two hundred residents were prostitutes. It was a nightly custom for patronage of the soiled doves to include not only the local boys, but miners from Creede, North Creede and Weaver, who tipped the hoistmen of the Last Chance and Commodore to lift them up to the wild, brawling and drunken delights of Bachelor.

The crash of silver in 1893 affected the whole Creede area. The population of Bachelor (according to the Colorado Business Directory) was down to eight hundred in 1896 and one hundred and fifty by 1910.

Unknown, 1910; D.P.L.

BACHELOR WAS FULL OF BRAWLING "BATCHERS"

The mining camp was already declining when this picture was taken. Its population had fallen from twelve hundred to one hundred and fifty.

Still Bachelor hung on as a town after that for a number of years. But the winters were so harsh, and transportation over the two-and-a-half mile road that climbed nearly two thousand feet up was so difficult that in the 'teens the last residents gave up. They moved down to Creede.

In 1960 there were only three cabins left standing on what was formerly Bachelor's residential street and a few remnants of the board-walk on its main street. Among the trees on the east side of the meadow, where Bachelor once lay, was a narrow picket-fenced grave, shaded by trees. A local story says that three bodies are buried there, one on top of the other, because of the difficulty of digging in the frozen ground the day after the tragedy that claimed all three.

It seems that a reforming minister, determined to alter the town's ways, moved to Bachelor at the height of its wickedness. He was a widower with a sixteen-year-old daughter. Hardly had they become settled in their cabin, than the girl caught bronchitis, and the minister was called down to Del Norte to conduct a funeral. As he left, the father cautioned the daughter to stay in the cabin, keep warm and admit no one, since he was afraid of the town's violent riff-raff.

When the minister returned three nights later, he was alarmed to see a saddle horse tied outside their door. He rushed inside and found a strange young man bending over his daughter who lay in bed. Whip-ping out a gun, the minister shot and killed the stranger. His daughter screamed and explained that the man was a doctor who had come to tend her. In her father's absence her bronchitis had deepened into pneumonia. Worn out by the effort of speaking, the girl fell back on her pillow and died shortly after. In remorse the minister turned the gun on himself. The three bodies were found together the next morning and buried amid swirling snow.

Bachelor's site is still tossed by storms. You can leave Creede with the top of your jeep down and the world bathed in sunshine to arrive in Bachelor forty-five minutes later beneath racing clouds and pelting rain. But its location has probably the most magnificent view of our selected ghost towns. It looks out across the Rio Grande Valley to Snowshoe Mountain and down the river to Wagon Wheel Gap. From here the gap shows more pictorially than from any other angle. On the return trip there is a perpendicular sight of Creede and a view of the continental divide with its mountains around Wolf Creek Pass and Summitville. This is a breathtaking experience when the autumn colors are at their height. Yes, you will find Bachelor unique for its view . . .

Spar City's location may also be seen on the Bachelor trip. It lies on the south side of the Rio Grande River up Lime Creek, about fourteen miles from Creede. It was originally named Fisher City after John Fisher who went prospecting in June, 1892, and found a rich float of silver and lead by climbing up Palo Alto Creek to the lower reaches of Fisher Mountain. The news electrified the latecomers to Creede, and a

MAIN STREET

This photo was taken fairly late in the afternoon and shows what is left of the main street—just a few timbers of the boardwalk. No matter what time of day you are in Bachelor you run the danger of bad weather.

Lonny Rogers, 1960

REMNANTS

These two houses used to ornament the residential street which ran parallel to the main street. The one in the rear has a covered walkway to the attached privy, a porch to the well, finely mortised and plastered walls and real flooring.

Lonny Rogers, 1960

rush ensued. By August the boomers had changed the original name to Spar City because of quantities of spar (or feldspar) in the area.

The population was between five hundred and one thousand, and cabins were going up fast. On September 24, the *Spar City Spark* started publication, and on October 29 a preliminary meeting of the town council was held. Six grocery stores, two restaurants, three livery stables, four saloons, two dance halls, a post office, a school and an assay office, besides the newspaper, were all going full tilt on the promise of great things to come. But the promise was never fulfilled. The Emma's ore proved too lean in values to ship. By the following year the Silver Panic cast a pall over all mining camps dependent on the white metal. Spar City lasted only through 1894 with people departing as hurriedly as they came. The editor of the *Spar City Spark* fled, leaving his fonts of type and issues of the paper. By 1895 the town's population mustered only twenty.

One of the prospectors who lingered on was Charles Brandt. On November 20, 1899, he filed on a homestead covering the entire townsite, and for a number of years Brandt was the sole owner. In 1908 backed by Charles King of Hutchinson, Kansas, he started the Bird Creek mine. Some ore was taken out; but it was the Emma's story over again. The ore was not rich enough for profitable operation.

On August 14, 1913, Charles King and other Kansas friends took over the townsite as a club for summer residents. They hired a caretaker for the property and set up rules for its thirty-five members. In 1955 the club, with its same limited membership, was changed to a corporation. Now a share of the stock goes with the sale of a cabin although the rules remain the same. No new cabins are permitted, and to buy an old cabin you must be passed on by the board of directors.

Spar City has a charming location with a view to the northwest of Bristol Head and beyond to the continental divide. It has three fishing and boating ponds and a community hall made from the old hotel. Here the annual banquet for members is held. The place is a going concern, aided by an informative history of the club, written by S. Horace Jones of Lyons, Kansas, designed to keep Spar City's traditions straight through the years of progress.

Some of the older members, like Dorothy Ruehling and Dr. O. W. Longwood, preserved copies of the *Spar City Spark*, the minutes of the town council, and other historical mementoes which were graciously shown to visitors interested in the town's development.

In 1960 Spar City was the least ghostly of our ghost towns despite the fact that once it had been a genuine ghost town for some fifteen years. Yet it found a place in our booklet on two counts—a mining town that never shipped a ton of ore and a boom camp that metamorphosed into a sedate well-ordered club. In each instance no stranger dispensation of fate could be imagined.

(Photos of Spar City on following two pages)

ODD GRAVE

In this quiet, pretty spot three bodies are said to lie, buried on top of each other as the result of an early tragedy. In the woods off to the left, or east, the old dump of the Last Chance mine shows alternating hues of amethysts and gold.

Orin Hargraves, 1960

O. W. Longwood, 1960

SPAR CITY HAS A CHARMING MAIN STREET

These views are both taken looking north toward the continental divide. The old hotel may plainly be seen as the only two-story structure of the group. Many of these original cabins have been added to but the members of the club are required to keep the additions in the style of the original architecture. The lower photo shows one of the three fishing and boating ponds and a pony for the children, curious and alert.

O. W. Longwood, 1960

ITS OLD HOTEL AND JAIL ARE CHERISHED

The main street was actually named North Street. The Spar City Spark for May 27, 1893 reported that the Free Coinage Hotel was being built and would have furniture from Denver. When it was changed into a Community Hall, bedroom doors on the second floor were removed which read "Rose—$1.00; Marie—$1.50; Ruth—$3.00," etc. The owner of the old jail has kept its original bars intact over one of the windows.

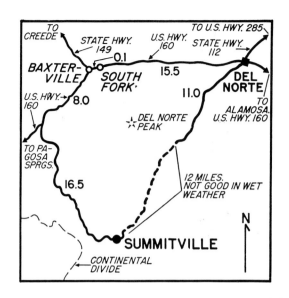

TO CREEDE
STATE HWY. 149
BAXTER-VILLE
0.1
U.S. HWY. 160
SOUTH FORK·
8.0
15.5
U.S. HWY. 160
STATE HWY. 112
TO U.S. HWY. 285
11.0
DEL NORTE
TO ALAMOSA.
U.S. HWY. 160
DEL NORTE PEAK
TO PA-GOSA SPRGS.
16.5
12 MILES.
NOT GOOD IN WET WEATHER
N
SUMMITVILLE
CONTINENTAL DIVIDE

From Del Norte

Summitville was next to the earliest of the San Juan mining camps. Yet gold is still tenaciously being mined there, and for that reason the town is unique.

In 1870 James L. Wightman went prospecting and placering up the Alamosa River from the San Luis Valley. When he came to rugged Wightman Fork Creek, he staked placer claims along its tumbling six-and-a-half mile length to Summitville, and then spent a snow-bound winter there at 11,000 feet altitude. From 1872 to '74 Summitville experienced a rush, and many lode claims were found on South Mountain. In 1875 the first amalgamation mill was erected and spearheaded decades of activity. By the late 1890's there were twelve separate stamp mills pounding noisily on Summitville ore.

In 1900 the mines closed down; operated again, 1911-1913; 1926-1931; and for about fifteen years after the mid-1930's. In 1948 two mills were vibrating: two stores and a large school were open, and sixty to seventy residences were fully occupied. The large boardinghouse had room for nearly three hundred men. At its height Summitville's maximum population was around fifteen hundred with about nine hundred men on the payroll. Lately the summer residents have been two.

In the early days three perilous toll roads led into town; the first from Jasper on the Alamosa; the second over the continental divide from Pagosa Springs, and the third from Del Norte. In 1960 the Forest Service was building a good new road that takes off a few miles above South Fork and will add to Summitville's accessibility.

Summitville's appearance may be stark and desecrated, but its gold is uniquely alive.

Joseph Collier, early 1870's; D.P.L.

NINETY-YEAR-OLD SUMMITVILLE WON'T DIE

Nearly ten million dollars have been extracted from its mines, which cover seven hundred-odd acres and stem from four main veins—the Tewksbury, Hidden, Copper and Little Annie. In 1960 the property was three-fourths owned by Mrs. George Garrey of Denver (daughter of A. E. Reynolds) and one-fourth by B. T. Poxon of Creede, and was leased to Jack Rigg whose crew commuted from the San Luis Valley.

Jack Rigg, 1960

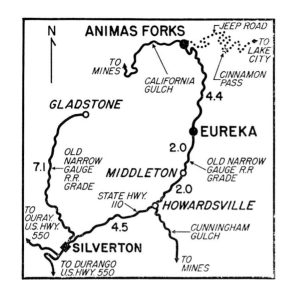

From Silverton

Eureka is the oldest of the San Juan camps, dating from 1860. That was the summer of the great placer excitement at Oro City (later Leadville). An enterprising prospector by the name of Charles Baker set out from Oro City on an exploration trip, backed in part by Samuel B. Kellogg. Kellogg had arrived in California Gulch (the site of Oro City) in May as a member of Horace A. W. Tabor's party and had become acquainted with Baker.

Baker and six companions made their way down the Arkansas River, over Poncha Pass, through the San Luis Valley, up the Rio Grande River, over Stony Pass, and down into the valley of the Animas River. Here they found a large park extending from just below Silverton, up past Howardsville to just beyond Eureka. They forthwith named it Baker's Park. They also found some placer gold which would yield about twenty-five cents to the pan. This seemed encouraging enough for others to follow, and a settlement was established, called Baker City (now Silverton). Their diggings and some brush shanties were nine miles above at what was later Eureka.

But the placer gold proved disappointing. Baker spent one terrible winter in his park and remained for the summer of 1861. Then he retreated to Fort Garland rather than attempt the hardship of a second winter. Here he heard about the Civil War and went home to Virginia to enlist in the Confederate army.

Years went by. Finally in 1874 Henry Gannett, leader of a detachment of the famous F. V. Hayden Geological Survey party, came down the Animas River, climbed over an enormous rockslide and "came out into a thick clump of trees in which were several log cabins, bearing

84

on a flaring sign board 'Eureka,' evidently intended for the name of a town that was expected to be, though what had been found there to suggest the name was not immediately apparent."

What was not apparent to Henry Gannett was the Sunnyside mine. It was staked in 1873 and had gathered around itself the cabins he encountered. The mine was so rich in gold that it operated continuously until 1931. Despite the richness of the Sunnyside, Eureka attained no greater rating in the Colorado Business Directory than "a small mining camp in the San Juans" until 1896 when Otto Mears' railroad, the Silverton Northern, was completed, and more people moved in for a time. Again there was a boom period in 1918 when the Sunnyside mill was rebuilt, and a large crew was hired. Eureka's population rose to two hundred and fifty.

Until 1931 no great change occurred. Then for six years, from 1931 to 1937, it was a ghost town. When the mine and mill re-opened in 1937, Eureka had about two years of new life only to die again because of a strike by the miners which the owners refused to settle. Again people moved away, and finally the Silverton Northern was sold and junked in 1942. By 1960 the town was almost leveled—and its unique jail towered alone—one of the most unusual buildings in Colorado. This odd jail gives Eureka its quality of uniqueness . . .

Five miles farther up the Animas is Animas Forks which supported three mills and was close to many good mines—the Iron Cap, Black Crow, Gold Prince, Eclipse and others. In 1877 it was a stagecoach stop on Otto Mears' toll road from Silverton to Lake City. According to George Crofutt's *Grip-Sack Guide of Colorado*, published in 1881, Animas Forks also had two stores, a hotel, a number of saloons and several small shops. Its population was then close to two hundred. But through the years its location at 11,200 feet altitude was extremely unfortunate because of snowslides. Dispatches frequently told of injuries and deaths to men only a short distance from town. Nevertheless, the Silverton Northern was extended to Animas Forks in 1904, and the town lived on in spurts until World War II.

In 1960 its jail, two of its mills, scattered outlying cabins, and a substantial residence with an impressive bay window were still standing. A number of erroneous tales have grown up around this house, saying that Thomas F. Walsh built it and that his daughter was born there. Actually Walsh's San Juan interests were all centered around Ouray and the Camp Bird mine.

But this house gives Animas Forks the uniqueness to enter our collection—a spot of pure folklore—Animas Forks. So don't believe what you hear while there!

(Photos of both towns on next two pages)

THE SUNNYSIDE WAS EUREKA'S MAINSTAY

The Sunnyside mine and mill were served by one of Otto Mears' three little railroads, the Silverton Northern. Gladstone, a similar mining camp to the west of Eureka and now also a ghost town, was served by its own railroad. The tall building at the right of both photos is the jail from which all the bars and bolts have recently been vandalized. The road that crosses below the dump at the right leads up to Animas Forks.

On these two pages the usual order of the "then" photo at the top of the page and the "now" photo at the bottom of the page has not been adhered to because of the size of the pictures. Eureka is at the top of both pages and Animas Forks at the bottom. Evalyn Walsh McLean testified in her book Father Struck It Rich that she was born in Denver on August 1, 1886 (see page 3). The local legend is quite erroneous.

EVALYN WALSH McLEAN DID NOT SLEEP HERE

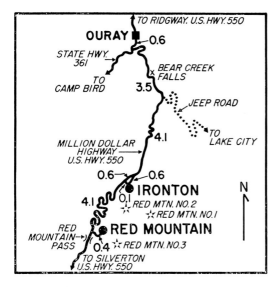

On the map:

TO RIDGWAY. U.S. HWY. 550

OURAY 0.6

STATE HWY. 361

TO CAMP BIRD

BEAR CREEK FALLS

3.5

JEEP ROAD

TO LAKE CITY

MILLION DOLLAR HIGHWAY U.S. HWY. 550

4.1

0.6 — 0.6

IRONTON

N

4.1 — 0.1

RED MTN. NO. 2

RED MTN. NO. 1

RED MOUNTAIN → PASS

RED MOUNTAIN

0.4 RED MTN. NO. 3

TO SILVERTON U.S. HWY. 550

From

Ouray

On the way over Red Mountain Pass two unusual ghost towns may be seen by slight northerly detours from the Million Dollar Highway. Originally known as the Rainbow Route, this highway was Otto Mears' toll road from Silverton to Ouray, and later the grade of his Silverton Railroad which ran as far as Ironton.

Red Mountain began first as a mining district in 1881 and then blossomed into two settlements, Red Mountain City and Red Mountain Town. There are also three separate Red Mountains to add to the confusion. But Red Mountain City, on the Silverton side of the pass, died an early death, and Red Mountain Town dropped the "town" a few years later. This left three mountains and a town with the identical name.

It was in the summer of 1881 that John Robinson and two companions found the Guston mine, according to Ernest Ingersoll in the 1885 edition of *Crest of the Continent.* The Guston's ore was low grade, but did have an excess of lead which was wanted by the Pueblo smelter. So the three continued working it. In August of the next year Robinson was hunting deer and carelessly picked up a small boulder. He was astonished at the weight, broke it open, and found solid galena. This led to the discovery of the Yankee Girl only a dozen feet below the surface.

A month later they sold their prospect hole for $125,000. The new owners had to pack the ore on burros all the way to Silverton, and still the ore yielded a profit of $50 a ton. The Yankee Girl's final production figures were around $5,000,000. But long before that, the mine caused a rush, and the town of Red Mountain was platted in June of 1883. By 1890 it had a population of six hundred, a water works, school house, weekly newspaper, saloons, business houses and shops—and dozens of stories of fluke discoveries.

The most sensational of these discoveries was that of the National Belle whose popularity and allure soon outshone that of the Yankee Girl. In 1883 some miners were working in an underground tunnel and accidentally broke through the foot wall into a cavity. One man took a candle and climbed down into an immense natural cavern. The flickering flame showed up effulgent pockets of gold and silver galenas, chlorides and carbonates—a veritable treasure cave. The National Belle became one of the most celebrated mines of the San Juans with a long, preciously-guarded life and production figures of close to $9,000,000.

Red Mountain was plagued by fires and was completely destroyed in June, 1895. It also changed its location once in 1886 to be close to the toll road, later the railroad. When trains began to reach Red Mountain in September, 1888, the depot had to be placed inside the wye because of the narrowness of the site.

In 1960 only the dump and shaft house of the National Belle gave any idea of the lively Red Mountain that once was—nonetheless a unique town because of its National Belle . . .

Ironton was three miles below Red Mountain and was as far as the Silverton Railroad could go because of the impossibility of laying rail in the precipitous confines of Uncompahgre Canyon on its way to Ouray. Ironton was founded in 1883 and platted in 1884 over a long oblong running beside Red Mountain Creek. Its main business was freighting and transportation for the many mines such as the Saratoga and Silver Belle, dotting the mountainsides above it. This was especially true after the Silverton Railroad began full operation in 1889. In 1890 its population was three hundred and twenty-two, around half that of its neighbor, Red Mountain.

As time went on, Ironton's more salubrious location won out. Ten years later Red Mountain had only thirty residents, and Ironton, seventy-one. Gradually they both melted away, although Ironton did not completely die until 1926 when the railroad track was removed.

In 1960 only ten or twelve houses remained. Two of them had been renovated by employees of the wealthy Idarado Mining Company which has consolidated all the mining activities of the Red Mountain district into one big operation. In addition the company has driven a long tunnel under the mountains to Pandora, close to Telluride. On the Red Mountain side Idarado's surface buildings are impressive enough to give hope that Colorado will make a comeback as a mining state.

Ironton won a place in our collection because when the Silverton Railroad was completed to this point, Otto Mears decided in celebration upon a new and unique railroad pass for his friends—a silver engraved watch fob.

Unknown, circa 1887; D.P.L.

THE NATIONAL BELLE MARKS RED MOUNTAIN

The upper photo was taken before the Silverton Railroad reached Red Mountain in 1888. The National Belle was already in profitable operation as can be seen from the size of the dump. In 1960 nothing remained of the town, and only the shaft house was standing. If you are traveling by jeep, there is a most picturesque alternate road into Red Mountain which leads out of the valley around the ridge to the right.

D.K.P., 1960

T. M. McKee, 1886; D.P.L.

IRONTON WAS THE RAILROAD TERMINUS

It was here that passengers on the Silverton Railroad transferred to a four-horse stage to continue their journey to Ouray. Actually the Silverton Railroad was later extended some two miles farther down the creek to Albany Gulch to pick up ore although Ironton was considered the real terminus. The railroad grade may be seen as it circles in the heavy timber at the left beyond this log cabin and to the town at right.

D.K.P., 1960

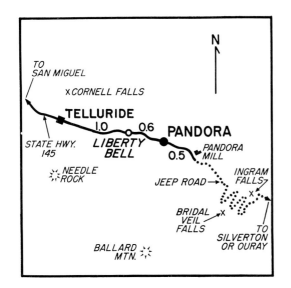

TO SAN MIGUEL

x CORNELL FALLS

TELLURIDE

STATE HWY. 145

LIBERTY BELL

1.0   0.6

PANDORA

PANDORA MILL

0.5

NEEDLE ROCK

JEEP ROAD →

INGRAM FALLS

BRIDAL VEIL FALLS

x

TO SILVERTON OR OURAY

BALLARD MTN.

N

From Tellu- ride

Pandora, two miles east of Telluride, was settled around 1881 and was briefly called Newport. But in August of that year, when a post office was established, the name was changed to Pandora. Undoubtedly this was because of the Pandora Mining Company which in 1883 already had a forty-stamp mill, a boardinghouse and offices in profitable operation, according to the Colorado Mining Directory of that year.

Pandora is unique in Colorado history for its annual snowslides, for its long aerial tramways, and at present for its amazing jeep trail.

As early as March 20, 1884, the *Rocky Mountain News* was reporting:

"The Pandora snowslide which comes down every winter, and which has been looked for for some time came down Monday, sweeping everything before it and making a total wreck of the Pandora sampling mills. Quite a number of Telluriders visited the effects of this slide this week. Some say it was not the Pandora slide, claiming it came over the Ajax Mine, following for some distance the former course of the Pandora slide. At all events, it was a terror."

But this devastating freak of nature did not discourage the pioneers. They rebuilt the mill, and through the years there has always been a large mill at Pandora. Twice it burned down but was always replaced. The Telluride Mines Company operated the mill up until 1956 when it was liquidated into the Idarado Mining Company, which also acquired the Tomboy Mines Company in the same year. Seventeen years after its inception Idarado thus consolidated all the big mining properties in the Pandora area under its own banner. These included the Pandora, Black Bear, Imogene, Barstow and the towers of the two spectacular trams into Pandora—the Tomboy from Savage Basin and the Smuggler Union. The Smuggler tramways landed at a site close to Ingram Falls from which ore was hauled to the mill past the Bridal Veil Falls and the present power plant down a two-thousand-foot cliff. In 1960 this old ore road had been converted into the last leg of Colorado's most fantastic jeep ride.

For many years Pandora was a sizable town. In its heyday the Rio Grande Southern Railroad had a spur from Telluride that passed through and reached the mill under stoutly built snow sheds. In 1960 the hauling of ore from the mill was done by trucks, and only three or four families were living there.

The actual site of Pandora is about half a mile down the San Miguel River from the mill, and its superb setting is now marred by two enormous tailings ponds between it and the river. But the town's backdrop of Ingram Peak with its two sets of falls, Bridal Veil and Ingram, cannot be matched anywhere in Colorado. Pandora is truly unique.

PANDORA'S SETTING IS SUPERB

In 1902 the population of Pandora was one hundred. Whatever its size, no town in Colorado can match its magnificent backdrop and jeep trail.

Joseph Byers, 1902-16; D.P.L.

MINING GHOSTS OF THE STORIED SAN JUANS

In saying farewell to the unique high-country places, you are left with many dramatic memories other than of towns alone. There are shaft houses or portal-houses like that of the Copper Vein mine at Summitville which provided Thomas M. Bowen with wealth to defeat Horace Tabor in his bid for the seven-year term for U.S. senator; or aerial tramways like the Tabasco mine's crossing Cinnamon Pass to its mill.

L'Envoi

If you have read this far, we hope that you have attempted one or more of the short trips. Perhaps you have done the whole suggested tour around Colorado and seen all forty-two of our selections. Whichever you have attempted, you must have come away awe-struck by the prodigious energy and enterprise of the pioneers. Their feats of transportation over villainous terrain, and of building shaft houses, dwellings and even towns on the face of cliffs or at the top of mountains, were so herculean as to seem incredible.

The pioneers' amazing accomplishments lie crumbling now. What cost them so much are largely regarded today as mere relics for curiosity or spots for souvenir-hunting—an attitude that raises my blood pressure to the danger mark. No one would think of chipping off a piece of tile from a fireplace in Spain or a bit of wood from a Tudor cottage in England. Yet they will do the equivalent in Colorado.

True, our past and our heritage are much closer to us here, but they should be no less dear. For my part, they are even dearer for being just around memory's corner and being almost within touch. When I stand on the rock dams of Lake Caroline (which my father named for me) and think of what effort a man would need to expend, working alone at 11,800 feet altitude with only a couple of hired workmen and a team of horses to build these dams, I cannot bear for one rock to be dislodged.

There were not only the rock dams of Lake Caroline but the concrete and rock dams of Ice, Ohman, Steuart, and Reynolds Lakes and the great earthen dam of Loch Lomond, the main lake of the reservoir system. I cannot remember the actual building of these dams; but I can remember the many horseback rides in later summers when my father and I went to check on the head gates and on what serious damage the severe winters had done to his engineering work.

And then there were those many shaft houses that I knew as a child and girl where my father was the consulting mining engineer. I cannot remember the shaft houses being built; but I can remember them later with the whir of the hoists, the sharp sound of the bell signals, and the clang of the primitive ore buckets and go-devils as they took us down the shafts. I can remember the speed of the go-devil in the Little Jonny mine near Leadville when in 1927 John Cortellini (then mayor of the town and superintendent of the mine) ushered us down with his courtly Italian manner. He expected me to be frightened at being brushed so rapidly past the crooked rock wall. But I thought it was fun.

I do not think it is fun today when I hear that the silent and deserted Little Jonny shaft house has been broken into and some of the machinery stolen. I know at what human and financial cost that machinery was put there. It should be left in peace until that rosy day when precious minerals and base metals are once again in demand.

Speaking of cost, no visitor to our collection of towns but must have wondered about finances. Only a gambler could understand them. It is my private contention that more money has been sunk into the mountains of Colorado than any wealth they have yielded up. But this is the practical and prosaic view of one who has heard too often about the millions that would pour in tomorrow when the vein widened out or when the drift was extended just ten more feet. Mining and narrow gauge railroading were for gamblers, and no one pretended otherwise. They had no illusions about its being an industry or a business. My father and his cronies always spoke of "the mining game."

But for a game it carried a deal of heartbreak. If you take time to look at the cemeteries of the mining towns, you cannot fail to notice the numbers of babies who could not survive in this harsh land nor the number of young men killed by accidents other than shootings, nor in the "Boot Hills" the number of unhappy young women who went the laudanum route. There is sadness, as well as serenity and romantic nostalgia, hanging in the aura of these high-country towns.

Memories of humor—raw pioneer humor—hang there also. The old-timers used their boundless energy for play and for practical jokes as well as for work. I remember a passage from the *Silver World* that was written about Eureka in April, 1877, which pictured their superhuman efforts at entertainment. A dance had been scheduled in one of the cabins, according to the correspondent who described the affair thus:

"Soon the damsels began to arrive, some on burros and some on foot. The music was provided by a fiddle and a banjo, and the ball opened with the 'San Juan Polka' which resembled a Sioux War dance . . . Soon the ironclads of the miners began to raise the dust of the floor so that before long it was impossible to tell what was what . . . Ground hog was the chief dish at the late supper which also served big ox, gravy, bacon, coffee, tea, and a large variety of pies and cakes. After this light repast the dance was resumed till morning."

* * *

And so, farewell, for the present. Let us hope that in the years to come both humans and nature will be kind to the high-country towns so that we may all continue to enjoy these reminders of a way of life that is now completely lost—a way of life that was the mainstay of Colorado for over half a century and is now only a mountain ghost.